Essential Elvis

by Peter Silverton

First published in Great Britain in 1997 by Chameleon Books
an imprint of Andre Deutsch Ltd
106 Great Russell Street
London WC1B 3LJ

Andre Deutsch Ltd is a subsidiary VCI plc

1 3 5 7 9 10 8 6 4 2

Printed and bound at Jarrold Book Printing.

A catalogue record for this book is available from the British Library
ISBN 0 23399245 6

the fifty

'I sing all sorts'.
Elvis to Sam Phillips' secretary Marion Keisker, on his first visit to Sun Studios, Memphis

As this book demonstrates, he sure did. Not all the songs Elvis recorded were great, but there was always something in the performance which made the fifty chosen numbers gathered together here, something special.

Author Peter Silverton has selected his personal, essential Elvis recordings, and his reasons for their inclusion are often startling, sometimes amazing and always engrossing. Worshippers at the altar of Elvis may well disagree with some of the songs included, but then, as The King himself sang, "Yoga is as Yoga does".

Enjoy.

Mal Peachey (editor)

Pictures

Pictorial Press; 6 (aged 15 with Betty McCann, who taught him to dance) 16 (with girlfriend Yvonne Lime), 19 (outside Graceland), 20, 26, 29 (with L-R , DJ Fontana, Scottie Moore, Bill Black) 30, 37, 44, 48 (with manager Colonel Tom Parker), 55, 58, 66, 78, 101.

Corbis-Bettmann; 11, 12, 33, 40 (what the cameras didn't show, taping the Ed Sullivan Show with the Jordanaires), 43, 52, 61 (Priscilla Beaulieu in Germany, writing to Elvis in America), 64, 69, 72, 93, 95, 109

Redferns; 5, 23, 74, 77, 81, 88, 105, 110, 112 (the televison room at Graceland).**Glenn A Baker Archives/Redferns;** 47

Alpha; 39, 50 (at home with Mama and Pop), 71, 82, 84 96, 98/99 (inside Graceland), 106 (Elvis' Colt 45, inscribed TCB - Taking Care of Business), 108 (Elvis' Drug Enforcement special agent badge), 114.

Rex Features; 24. **Camera Press;** 117. **Janus van Helfteren;** 118-121.

RCA Album sleeves; 10" Good Rockin' Tonight, 15; Reconsider Baby on blue vinyl, 63; The Comeback TV Special, 85; 1969: Year In Review, 102; The Memphis Album, 122; The Sun Collection, Elvis Is Back, 123.

Picture research; Odile Schmitz

The author and publishers have made every reasonable effort to contact all copyright holders. Any errors that may have occurred are inadvertent and anyone who for any reason has not been contacted is invited to write to the publishers so that a full acknowledgement may be made in subsequent editions of this work.

(A is for Aaron)

Elvis' middle name, which his mother misspelled as Aron on his birth certificate, but was finally corrected to Aaron on his gravestone.

That's All Right (Mama)
Written by: **Arthur Crudup**
Recorded: **5 July 1954, Sun Records, 605 Union Avenue, Memphis**
First released: **19 July 1954, coupled with Blue Moon Of Kentucky**

The moment. Not that anyone knew it at the time. Oh, old Sam Phillips had an idea. He'd started a record company in a little street corner studio on the edge of Memphis. Not far from the university, it was a long way east, down Union Avenue, from the city's economic and political power base close by the Mississippi River. In the early 1950s, Sam Phillips was cutting hits with the wildest, blackest blues and R&B singers he could find. Future big names like Howlin' Wolf, BB King, Ike Turner and strange, fleeting characters like Jackie Brenston — whose Rocket 88 is often cited as 'the first rock and roll record' — and guitarist Pat Hare who sang I'm Gonna Murder My Baby and then did just that a few years later. Sam Phillips' first real hit was Bear Cat by Rufus Thomas, an 'answer record' to the original R&B version of a song Elvis himself would later make world-famous — Big Mama Thornton's Hound Dog. It hit number three on the R&B charts. Right after that, he nearly hit the bigtime with Just Walking In The Rain, cut by the Prisonnaires, a quartet of inmates in the Tennessee State Prison. But the hit came three years later, with a version by Johnnie 'The Nabob Of Sob' Ray.

It wasn't the first time Elvis had recorded at Sun. Sam Phillips also ran a vanity recording business. Nearly a year earlier in August 1953, Elvis had turned up, paid his $3.98 plus tax for a two-sided acetate, and recorded two pop songs, accompanying himself on rudimentary guitar. My Happiness is a gloopy, sentimental ballad that Elvis had practised again and again at home, a 1948 pop hit for Jona and Sandra Steele. It is completely impossible to see in it what the future would hold.

The other song is even odder. That's When Your Heartaches Begin was first recorded in 1941 by the Inkspots, a smooth, black vocal group. Syrupy and seemingly sentimental, it appears to address the problems of troilism. 'Love is a thing you never can share/When you bring a friend into your love affair/That's when your heartaches begin.' What made it an even stranger choice was that Elvis himself claimed he'd cut the two tracks as a birthday gift for his beloved Mama — an unlikely idea as her next birthday was not for another eight months. You can hear the future in this side.

The timbre of his voice, particularly on the word 'share', foreshadows the early Sun sides. The reverent hokiness of the recitative in the middle of the song prefigures both the cringeingly fake false start on Milkcow Blues Boogie — 'Hold it, fellas, that don't move me. Let's get real, real gone for a change' — and the lush, bombastic sincerity of 1970s show-stoppers like If I Can Dream.

The stupid joke at the end — he says 'that's the end' as if it is part of the song, then just stops singing — is all of a piece with the man who, in three or so years, would headline at Las Vegas and fail to wow the crowd with jokes about songs called Heartburn Motel and Get Out Of The Stables, Grandma, You're Too Old To Be Horsing Around.

Those two songs, though, were personal. That's All Right (Mama) is the business. Over the year, Elvis had charmed and impressed Sam Phillips' secretary, Marion Keisker. Eventually she persuaded Sam to record him and Sam put him together with two older, experienced country musicians, guitarist Scotty Moore and bassist Bill Black. 'When I first met him,' said Scotty Moore, 'I think he was dressed in pink pants with a stripe down the side, and he had a ducktail haircut. But he seemed to know any song you could name.'

The three of them rehearsed together on the Sunday, Independence Day 1954, and went into the studio the following night. They tried a pop song, the four-year-old Bing Crosby hit, Harbor Lights, and a five-year-old country standard, I Love You Because.

Neither worked that well, though, and they were just getting ready to call off the session when Elvis remembered an eight-year-old blues song, Arthur 'Big Boy' Crudup's That's All Right. A couple of years later, Elvis told a journalist: 'I used to hear Arthur Crudup bang his box the way I do now, and I said that if I ever got to the place where I could feel all that Arthur felt, I'd be a music man like nobody ever saw.'

Crudup (pronounced to rhyme with brewed-up) recorded his song in Chicago, above Eli's Pawn Shop on South State Street. A Delta bluesman from Forest, Mississippi, he was a sharecropper and bootlegger — as was Muddy Waters — who journeyed north a couple of times a year to make recordings for Lester Melrose's Bluebird Records. He got $75 to $200 a side and not a cent in royalties. Understandably, he was bitter: 'I was making everybody rich and I was poor.' When he died, in 1970, he was still trying to get recompense and the rights to his own songs from their publishers, Hill & Range. A sour irony — they were also Elvis' publishing house.

On that Monday night in Memphis, though, Elvis picked up his guitar — a Martin D-18 which was sold for $152,000 at Christies in 1993 — and began to play Crudup's blues. Bill joined in, then Scotty — no drummer, notice. Sam Phillips recorded it, helping refine and focus it as the evening wore on. Somewhere along the way, it lost two of Crudup's verses, finally clocking in at a couple of bars short of two minutes. It also gained a third word in its title, becoming That's All Right (Mama) for the first time — an intriguing change, given Elvis's Oedipal tendencies.

Sam Phillips took a copy to the most important local dee-jay, Dewey Phillips (no relation) whose studios were downtown, close to the Peabody Hotel, now renowned for its ducks, but then the spot where Memphis power-brokers sipped their after-work drinks. Six years earlier, in his memoirs Where I Was Raised And Born, David L Cohn famously wrote, 'The Mississippi

That's All Right (Mama)

Delta begins in the lobby of the Peabody Hotel in Memphis and ends on Catfish Row in Vicksburg'. That other, even more famous local writer, William Faulkner, was so struck by this line that he later borrowed it for a travel piece on Mississippi in Holiday magazine.

Dewey took the record, played it on his show on the Thursday night and got such a great response that he played it again, and invited Elvis in to talk about it — or rather, it is generally agreed, to prove to his listeners that Elvis was a young white boy rather than an old black bluesman. Released ten days later, it was a hit — albeit a minor regional one. A career was launched, one whose end would be marked by a comment from the President. 'Elvis Presley's death,' said Jimmy Carter, 'deprives our country of a part of itself.'

If the story sounds too pat to be true, it's the one that all the participants have told over the years. And its Genesis-like quality fits neatly with Dave Marsh's overexcited description of That's All Right (Mama) as a 'Rosetta stone' of pop, and with something John Lennon said: 'Before Elvis, there was nothing.'

Strangely, although Crudup's original That's All Right wasn't a hit on first release in 1946, it had its moment in the sun two years later — as a result of the format wars between Columbia (now Sony) and RCA (who'd bought out Bluebird). Since their beginnings, in 1900, records had always been ten inches in diameter and spun at 78 rpm. Then, in 1948, Columbia introduced the twelve-inch 'microgroove' spinning at 33 rpm. RCA hit back with Project Madame X, the bizarre cover name for their seven-inch, 45 rpm 'donut disc' which reached the market in 1949.

As a marketing gimmick, RCA put each of their product lines on different-coloured vinyl. Country was green. Classical was red. Children's records were yellow. And, as blue was already allocated to pop music, the world's first 45 rpm rhythm and blues side was an RCA reissue of Arthur Big Boy Crudup's That's All Right — on orange vinyl.

Although Elvis' version of That's All Right (Mama) launched a career, it remained unknown by the world at large, and stayed that way for a long time. Its first album appearance was not until For LP Fans Only, released in 1959 as stopgap product while Elvis was in the army, which proved to be his least successful record to that date, climbing no higher than number 19 in the US charts.

But the song's real invasion of the public consciousness came only in 1975 when UK RCA released — at budget price — The Sun Collection. Collated and annotated by The NME's Roy Carr, it was the first piece of Elvis curatorship. It brought together all the then-known Sun recordings (in their original mono), and adding a few numbers previously available only on a Dutch bootleg, Good Rocking Tonight — which also included a fabulous argument between Sam Phillips and Jerry Lee Lewis over whether the latter was committing blasphemy by recording Great Balls Of Fire. *ep*

(B is for Blue)

On the night Elvis was born, his father Vernon stepped out into the backyard and saw the skies were ringed in blue light. As a young boy, Elvis discovered that if he stared at the moon long enough, a blue ring would appear round it. Years later, he decided that blue was a colour with deep spiritual significance. The flip side of his first single was Blue Moon Of Kentucky. He also recorded Blue Suede Shoes, Blue Christmas, Blue Moon, Blue Eyes Crying In The Rain, Blue River, Blueberry Hill, A Mess Of Blues, Mean Woman Blues, Indescribably Blue, Milkcow Blues Boogie, Something Blue, Good Time Charlie's Got The Blues, Steamroller Blues and When My Blue Moon Turns To Gold Again. He cut GI Blues and Blue Hawaii — both of which are, of course, the title tracks of entire movies with the same name. And Moody Blue was the title track of his very last LP. By way of colour comparison, he didn't record a single song with red, orange or purple in its title.

In fact, the complete list of his other colour-significant recordings is: one black — Long Black Limousine; one yellow — The Yellow Rose Of Texas; one white — White Christmas; and two green — A Little Bit Of Green and The Green, Green Grass Of Home. Just five in total, compared to eighteen for blue alone. An article in the Rainbow Earth Dwelling Society Newsletter, as recorded by 'Tubbs Gillis' in Magical Blend magazine, reveals that Elvis believed he'd had a previous life on a blue planet orbiting a blue sun in the Pleiades Dogstar system.

In his essay, Elvis In Death, Nick Tosches wrote that, for some time before Elvis' death, he'd thought of him not as a real person but as 'an all-American demi-god who dwelt, enthroned between Superman and the Lone Ranger, in the blue heaven of the popular imagination'.

The colour of the pyjamas in which he died? Blue. As was the shirt and tie in which he was buried.

Blue Moon Of Kentucky
Written by: **Bill Monroe**
Recorded: **6 July 1954, Sun**
First released: **flipside of That's All Right (Mama), 19 July 1954**

The famous leg twitch started here. And Rockabilly. And tape echo so deep you'd think they were recording in the caves of Malabar.

According to various people's versions, Blue Moon Of Kentucky was recorded either right before its A-side, That's All Right (Mama), or right after it, or the following night, or nearly a week later on the weekend starting 9 July — the most recent revision, convincingly made by Peter Guralnick in Last Train To Memphis.

That's All Right (Mama) had already been played on the radio by Dewey Phillips — fourteen times on the spin according to legend. It was an obvious hit in waiting. But it needed a b-side and nothing Sam Phillips had recorded up to this point pleased him. So he called a new session for the Friday — which stretched into the weekend. As Scotty Moore tells it, 'We spent three or four nights trying to get a back side . . . then Bill [Black] jumped up and started clowning, beating on his bass and singing Blue Moon Of Kentucky in a high falsetto voice, more or less mimicking Bill Monroe. And Elvis started banging on the guitar, playing rhythm and singing, and I joined in and it just gelled.'

The author of Blue Moon Of Kentucky, Bill Monroe, was known as 'The father of Bluegrass music', a Country style which was a mixture of banjo, fiddle-playing and harmony singing. Bluegrass emerged during the Second World War, not — as is often claimed — full-born and folkily authentic from the hills of Kentucky but as one of the first Southern Pop forms. Like any other Pop it is a hybrid — the banjo came from Africa, the guitar from southern Europe, the fiddle from Northern Europe and the basics of many of the songs from old English 'Folk' numbers.

Kentuckian Monroe, leader of the Blue Grass Boys, added his own particular favourite rhythm to the mix — the waltz. That is, he mixed a taste of late nineteenth Century Austro-Hungarian Empire into the pot. And his eclecticism was

appreciated. Kentucky Waltz was a big hit and so was his Blue Moon Of Kentucky, originally one of the sweetest waltzes ever recorded.

Which Elvis' version certainly isn't. It's in 4/4 and it's a Country song, yes, but you can't say it's Country music. It's as loud as R&B, for a start. As Elvis himself put it, he bangs on his guitar 'like it was the lid of a garbage can'. At the end of one early take — which has nothing like the crunch of the final one — you can hear Sam Phillips say: 'Hell, that's different. That's a Pop song now.' Even Bill Monroe himself understood what Elvis, Sam, Scotty and Bill were after, and what they'd achieved. Two months later, in early September, impressed by Elvis' iconoclastic treatment of his icon-like song, Bill Monroe went into a Nashville studio and recut his own song in 4/4 time.

Blue Moon Of Kentucky marked the start of Elvis' fascination with the colour blue. On record, anyway — the personal fascination dated way back.(See B is for blue, opposite). *ep*

Tomorrow Night
Written by: **Sam Coslow, Will Gross**
Recorded: **10 September 1954, Sun**
First released: **Elvis For Everyone album, 1965**

Tomorrow Night was a song Elvis sang all the time in the year before he first recorded. His then girlfriend Dixie Locke recalled how, on hot summer nights, he'd sit on her porch singing it — and that, later, he played her Lonnie Johnson's original version. It was good, she thought, but it wasn't as good as Elvis'. (Another history has Elvis discovering it on the flipside of Lavern Baker's Tweedle Dee, which he also played onstage in the Sun years.)

Lonnie Johnson is certainly the most underacknowledged figure in mid-twentiethth century blues-based popular music. Born in New Orleans (in either 1894 or 1899), he recorded blues sides as early as the mid-1920s, worked (and dallied) with the blues diva Bessie Smith and played with Duke Ellington and on Louis Armstrong's Savoy Blues. In 1925, he was signed to Okeh records by Jesse Stone, a black man from Kansas whose grandfather bought the first Cadillac in the state, at the 1904 St Louis World's Fair who was taught assonance by Cole Porter and who later wrote Shake, Rattle And Roll for Big Joe Turner and Money Honey for the Drifters — both of which Elvis covered.

In What Was The First Rock'N'Roll Record?, the authors claim that Johnson's sophisticated, jazzy guitar style, heavy on 'single-string vibrato' and 'ninth chords', was a defining influence on Delta bluesman Robert Johnson, French Gypsy jazz guitarist Django Reinhardt and black American jazz guitarist Charlie Christian. One of the first to master the electric guitar, Christian was a major figure in the development of bebop. Both Reinhardt and Christian in turn influenced BB King who claimed: 'Lonnie Johnson is my idol.'

Johnson also impressed a Scottish banjo player called Tony Donegan so much that he changed his first name to Lonnie in honour of his idol, and invented skiffle — the British musical style now best recalled as inspiring John Lennon's first band, the Quarrymen.

Johnson recorded Tomorrow Night in 1947, for Syd Nathan's Cincinnati-based King label, later home to James Brown. The song, already eight years old, was written by Sam Coslow, who also wrote My Old Flame and Will Grosz, who wrote On The Isle Of Capri, for Horace Heidt And His Orchestra. Johnson's light, plaintive voice made it a number one R&B hit.

It's a typical Elvis love song, a slightly anguished plea, which RCA first released in 1965 on Elvis For Everyone, drenched in strings and backing vocals. The simple directness of his vocal only became clear in 1985 when it was released in its original form – which Sam Phillips was never happy with – because there is a space where the guitar solo was clearly meant to be. *ep*

Good Rockin' Tonight

Written by: **Roy Brown**
Recorded: **10 September 1954, Sun**
First released: **coupled with I Don't Care If The Sun Don't Shine, 25 September 1954**

Of all the many extraordinary claims made about Elvis since his death, Charlie Feathers' must be the most revisionist. Co-writer of the flipside of Elvis' last Sun single, I Forgot To Remember To Forget, Feathers was a minor rockabilly star in the 1950s — not that there have ever been any major rockabilly stars. Like other rockabillies, Charlie Feathers took the musical innovations of Elvis' Sun sides and set them in stone. His best single was One Hand Loose, with its mysterious couplet, 'Give me one hand loose/And I'll be satisfied'.

But his greatest moment came in 1990, in an interview. 'Not too many people know it,' he said, 'but Gladys [Elvis' mother] took a trip to Florida without Vernon [Elvis' father] and was carryin' on with a coloured fellow down there and was pregnant right after. Nope, Vernon ain't his daddy. No sir.'

It's true that Elvis had Native American, as well as Scottish, ancestors and that there was sometimes a strange duskiness about his skin tone. At 11 years of age, he was photographed with slicked hair and wearing a shirt with a collar the size of the state of Tennessee: he certainly looks a whole lot more Negroid than the supposedly black founder of the Blues, Charley Patton, ever did.

And it must be said that Charlie Feathers' claim puts a whole new complexion — ouch! — on Sam Phillips' famous statement: 'If I could find a white man who had the Negro sound and the Negro feel, I could make a billion dollars.'

But Elvis' whiteness has often been used as a critical stick to beat him. It's a notion whose most extreme expression was the basic aesthetic premise of Goldman's biography: not only did Elvis steal his music from black people and then whiten it down, to vast profit, thereby debasing its artistic integrity; but also Elvis' very whiteness precluded artistic integrity in his chosen musical form — that is, Elvis was no good *because* he was white.

Good Rockin' Tonight, Elvis' second single, does for that thesis in just two minutes and twelve seconds. It had already been an R&B hit twice. It's not just that Elvis' version is better, though it is. It goes further than that. The 'blackness' of a piece of blues or R&B is traditionally characterised by its rhythmic drive, loudness, aggression, melismatic singing (basically, more than one note per vowel sound) and overall sexiness. By which criteria, Elvis' version of Good Rockin' Tonight is by far the 'blackest'.

It was written and first recorded in 1948 by Roy Brown, a New Orleans blues shouter. The song's joyous opening call — 'Well, I heard the news, there's good rockin' tonight' — came from the nationally broadcast wartime programmes of Gabriel Heatter, who'd begin his 'happy news' show with the announcement, 'Good evening, America, there's good news tonight'. Not that this conceit's first musical appearance was on Good Rockin' Tonight. No, it originally cropped up — as did something very similar to Good Rockin' Tonight's tune — on (black) Sy Oliver's 1946 minor pop hit (Ah Yes) There's Good Blues Tonight. Nor does it stop

there. Sy Oliver had already recorded the tune in 1941, as Yes Indeed, with the (white) Tommy Dorsey band. And, as it's very much a Gospel tune, it's highly likely that Oliver himself 'borrowed' it from an as yet uncovered source.

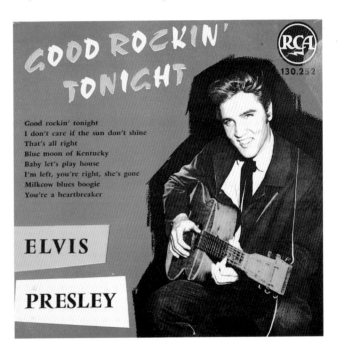

The second recording of Good Rockin' Tonight, by Wynonie Harris, was the big hit. A charming chancer with a voice as rough as a bear's bum, Wynonie Harris simplified and livened up the song, taking it to the top of the R&B charts.

Elvis — together with Scotty and Bill — finished off what Wynonie Harris started, giving Sam Phillips that 'Negro feel' he had been searching for. A moment and a place had collided. The blues had come to Memphis in 1910, when WC Handy had brought them up from the Mississippi Delta and written Memphis Blues as the mayoral campaign tune of a Mr Crump who was duly elected. He ruled the city with an iron and corrupt rod till his death in 1954. It was also the year of the Brown versus the Board Of Education of the State of Mississippi judgement, the first step of the long battle for racial integration which raged across the southern states right through to the early 1970s.

Put that way, Elvis' emergence doesn't seem quite so unexpected. Sam Phillips put it best, telling Peter Guralnick in Last Train To Memphis: 'The lack of prejudice on the part of Elvis Presley had to be one of the biggest things that ever could have happened to us. It was almost subversive, sneaking around through the music. But we hit things a little bit, don't you think? I went out into this no-man's land and I knocked the shit out of the colour line.' *ep*

I'm Left, You're Right, She's Gone

Written by: **Stanley Kesler, Bill Taylor**
Recorded: **10 December 1954, Sun**
First released: **flipside of Baby, Let's Play House, April 1955**

I'm Left, You're Right, She's Gone, the flip of his third single, was the first occasion Elvis got to record a song specially written for him. Till then, they'd all been covers of other artists' material. I'm Left, You're Right, She's Gone was by Stan Kesler, the steel guitarist with the Snearly Ranch Boys who Sam Phillips took to using on sessions in the winter of 1954 — Kesler also played on early pre-rockabilly singles by Carl Perkins, Charlie Feathers and Warren Smith. Even when he wasn't working there, he'd hang around the studio — which is how he came to hear that Sam Phillips was looking for original songs for Elvis. He went straight home and wrote I'm Left, You're Right, She's Gone, with fellow Snear Ranch Boy, trumpet-player Bill Taylor. The melody, he has said, is based on a contemporary advert for Campbell's Soup.

Elvis was given a basic demo of the song by Kesler — who wrote four other numbers for Elvis, including I Forgot To Remember To Forget, the flipside of the next Sun single. But that demo was only a starting point, as you can clearly hear on an early take of the song which was first issued in the mid-1970s on a Dutch bootleg, mistitled My Baby's Gone. Six more takes appeared on The Complete Sun Sessions. The difference between the early tentative versions and the one finally issued offers a clear demonstration of how Sun's real million dollar quartet — Elvis, Scotty, Bill and Sam Phillips — worked on and developed a song. The early take is a fine, slow, brooding arrangement, more Country than anything Elvis was recording at the time. By the final version, the four of them have turned it into a pop song. *ep*

(C is for Costello)

The other Elvis, who has never recorded a Presley song, though he did play Little Sister in his live shows for a while, introducing it as something by 'an unknown singer from Tupelo, Mississippi. And he did use some of the same musicians as EP. Guitarist James Burton, keyboard player Larry Knechtel, bassist Jerry Scheff and drummer Ron Tutt formed the Confederates, who appeared in live EC shows of the late 1980s and on 1987's King Of America album. Scheff was also on 1989's Spike. Burton, Scheff and Knechtel appear on 1995's Kojak Variety. And Tutt is on 1985's The People's Limousine which EC recorded under the pseudonym of the Coward Brothers (with T-Bone Burnett). EC's father, Ross MacManus, did however sing many EP songs. As the singer with the Joe Loss band in the 1950s, Mr MacManus sang whatever was a hit that week — some songs were even recorded, for cheap cover-version EPs for sale only in Woolworth's.

Baby, Let's Play House

Written by: **Arthur Gunter**
Recorded: **5 February 1955, Sun**
First released: **c/w I'm Left, You're Right, She's Gone, April 1955**

This is where the hiccups began. And this is how: 'Oh, b-b-b-baby, baby, b-b-b-baby, baby baby. Come, back baby, come. Come back, baby. I wanna play house with you'.

Baby, Let's Play House was a total reinvention of a recent R&B hit by the otherwise obscure Arthur Gunter which, in turn, owed more than a little to Eddy 'The Tennessee Plowboy' Arnold's 1951 Country tune, I Want To Play House With You. (As ever with pop music, the closer you stare, the more complex the racial mix gets.)

Elvis shouts 'Hit it!' and Scotty Moore plays straight blues in a style that set the pattern for a million Heavy Metal solos. Where Gunter sang 'you may have religion', Elvis took the lyric into his own world — 'you may drive a pink Cadillac', with a heavy emphasis on the 'pink'. He also gave a clear account of the overwhelming jealousy that would dominate and warp his emotional life: 'I'd rather see you dead, little girl, than to see you with another man.'

Unsurprisingly, it was Elvis' first real hit, reaching number ten on the national Country charts. Just as unsurprisingly, its invitation to premarital sex caused the first moral outrage about Elvis. *ep*

Mystery Train
Written by: **Little Junior Parker**
Recorded: **11 July 1955, Sun**
First released: **flipside of I Forgot To Remember To Forget, August 1955**

Doc Pomus, with his partner Mort Shuman, wrote a heap of hits for Elvis in the early 1960s, but he first heard Elvis in New York in 1955, he says. 'I was singing in this joint on 70th Street called the Musicale when I heard this record on the jukebox called Mystery Train. And I just couldn't believe it. It sounded like somebody just came out of the swamp.'

Elvis' fourth Sun single, Mystery Train was an updating, an improvement even, of an earlier Sun recording of the song by its writer, Little Junior Parker. That in turn is an adaptation of Worried Man Blues, a 'folk' tune first recorded in the 1930s by the Carter Family, a white Gospel and Country outfit whose musical lineage extends to current Nashville star, Carlene Carter. While Parker's Mystery Train is a smooth R&B tune, Elvis' version has the touch of otherworldly mania the lyrics seem to merit — they tell of the singer's woman being carried off by the mystery train of the title. (By the by, the train has sixteen coaches — and Elvis' funeral cortege had sixteen limos.)

Parker was a local boy, from West Memphis, a small city on the far side of the Mississippi in Arkansas where the looser licensing laws encouraged the development of bar bands. Parker's outfit, the seven or eight-strong Blue Flames, was a regular on Beale Street, the centre of black nightlife in Memphis. Parker was also part of the loose grouping known as the Beale Streeters, which included soul blues singer Bobby Bland and BB King, then best known as a local dee-jay.

By the time Elvis, Scotty and Bill came to record Mystery Train — augmented by Johnny Bernero on drums — they had been playing together for more than a year. You can hear it in the track's lightness of touch and concentrated offhandness.

It was Elvis' last Sun single and, out of everything he recorded, it has inspired more of what can only be called respect. Jim Jarmusch used it as the title for his film about Memphis. When the Band recorded it, Robbie Robertson was moved to write a whole new verse which meshed sweetly with the original. Greil Marcus took it as the title for his first book — subtitled Images Of America In Rock'n'Roll Music. Paul Simon said it was his 'favourite record of all time'. And Sam Phillips himself said: 'It was the greatest thing I ever did on Elvis.'

Tryin' To Get To You

Written by: **Rose Marie McCoy, Margie Singleton**
Recorded: **11 July 1955, Sun**
First released: **Elvis Presley LP, March 1956**

Although it was not released until 1956 on Elvis' first album, Tryin' To Get To You was the last complete master he cut with Sam Phillips, at the same session which produced both sides of his last single — I Forgot To Remember To Forget and Mystery Train. It was one week over a year since he'd recorded That's All Right (Mama). Now he was a regional star with hit records. The intention was to issue Tryin' To Get To You as the follow-up to Mystery Train.

But before a suitable flipside could be recorded, Elvis was off and away, to RCA Records, New York.

Although it's an R&B tune — first recorded in distant obscurity by the Eagles, a group from Washington DC — Tryin' To Get To You is the first time Elvis' Gospel roots appear on a record. The church is in his singing — impassioned and reverential at the same time — in the piano-playing by Elvis himself, and in the lyrics which basically put a woman where the words 'Jesus' or 'Lord' would normally go. Yet somehow there is no sense of blasphemy — something that another Memphis Flash, Al Green, put right twenty years later when he made a career out of a similar conflation of sex and religion.

Elvis' affection for the song

(D is for Dilaudid)

Pharmaceutical morphine in pill form. Elvis liked Dilaudid. He also liked Amytal, Quaaludes, Dexedrine, Biphetamine and Percodan — all pills and capsules prescribed to him by Dr George Nichopoulos. Not that this meant Elvis was a junkie. Rather, as many fine minds have pointed out, he was a heavy user of pharmaceutical preparations — addicted not to 'proscribed drugs' but 'prescribed drugs'. (Yes, it's true, a millennium ago, these same fine minds were engaged on debating the How Many Angels To A Pin Head? question.) In the last two and a half years of Elvis' life, Dr Nick wrote him scripts for 19,000 hits of the drugs he liked. 'The worst case of indiscriminate oversubscribing I have ever seen in my investigations for the State of Tennessee', said a local prosecutor on Geraldo Rivera's 13 September, 1979 US TV report, The Elvis Cover–Up, which exposed the extent and range of Elvis' multiple drug abuse.

Elvis Alphabet

is shown by his decision to perform it on his TV comeback special — with great ease and, if anything, even more conviction. Then he often did seem more comfortable with the sacred than the secular. It is claimed he was involved with the plans to build a Gospel Music Hall Of Fame — though it's hard to imagine quite what the organisers would have made of his taste for Kahlil Gibran and his appointing a Hollywood hairdresser as a spiritual adviser.

However, JD Sumner, leader of Elvis' vocal backing group in the 1970s' has stated that Elvis would have become a full-time Gospel singer if he'd lived another six months.

Maybellene
Written by: **Chuck Berry**
Recorded: **August 1955, live show, Municipal Auditorium, Shreveport, Louisiana**
First released: **on The Complete 50s Masters, 1992**

Not only by far the best recorded taste of the very early Elvis shows, but also a beguiling example of racial switcharounds. Played by young (white) men like it's an ancient (black) Country blues. Written by (black) Chuck Berry. Based on Ida Red by the (white) Bob Wills And The Texas Playboys who played Western Swing (white tunes, black rhythms). A hit on the Chicago blues and R&B label, Chess (white-owned, black roster). Recorded in the deep (white) South on the Louisiana Hayride, a major (white) live Country music radio show — the same year that, not at all far away in Mississippi, 14-year-old (black) Emmett Till was murdered for asking 21-year-old (white) Carolyn Bryant for a date.

It was around this time that Elvis' first manager, Bob Neal, started telling Elvis that his music was too 'coloured'. Soon after Elvis was managed by Colonel Tom Parker (white, Dutch, illegal immigrant, real name Andreas Cornelius van Kuijk).

Maybellene was Chuck Berry's first record. Made earlier that year in late May, and released in July, it was a big hit, topping the (black) R&B charts for eleven weeks, and reaching number five on the (white) pop charts. It's the first teenage car song, which Chuck Berry, then a 30-year-old trained beautician, originally played with a plodding Country rhythm. Willie Dixon, effectively Chess Records' artistic director, told Chuck it should be a blues. Chuck threw a mood, stormed out of Chess' Chicago offices and back to his home town of St Louis — though he was so broke that he had to sell some of his blood to a blood bank to finance the journey. A few weeks later, he called Chess and sang the new bluesy version. 'That made it a mixture of Country & Western and Blues,' said Willie Dixon. 'Which is Rock and Roll.'

Although Elvis' version is billed as featuring both Bill Black and Scotty Moore, all you can hear is the voice — poised, delicate, like it's running over hot coals— and Scotty's ringing, piercing electric guitar. He plays as far from his own Country roots as it's possible to imagine. Elvis shouts 'Hit it!' and Scotty plays a pure Blues solo which out-Chucks Chuck, just one note hit again and again — if Phillip Glass had been born in the Mississippi Delta he could well have sounded like this. Chuck's playing on his own Maybellene, by the way, quotes the Floyd Murphy solo on Junior Parker's original version of Mystery Train.

The crowd loved it, of course. Elvis and his band had been Saturday night Hayride regulars for about a year — he got $18 a show, the others $12 each. At the start, the audience had been regular, grown-up Country fans. By now, though, word had got around and every week the place was swamped by teenage fans of Elvis, who not only didn't care that he was singing black Pop hits, but had very possibly bought their own copies of Maybellene.

Even more than That's All Right, this was the moment black and white Pop came together again, after having gone their separate ways at the turn of the century. Its scant one minute fifty eight seconds probably says as much about the racial complexities of the post-war Deep South as any Faulkner book. It certainly spoke to a far wider (and mostly likely less liberal) audience, at the very time the whole region was about to plunge into a decade of white supremacist violence.

With its attempt to reverse a nation's racial divide through song it succeeded, innocently and musically, in making the same point Elvis seemed to be reaching for, far more self-consciously, more than a decade later. Both the song with which he closed his 'comeback' TV special, If I Can Dream, and An American Trilogy came very close to grandiosity. Very close. Which is something you'd never get from Chuck Berry. He is, after all, the man who wrote — or rather, adapted from a Folk source — My Ding A Ling. *ep*

Heartbreak Hotel

Written by: **Tommy Durden, Mae Axton**
Recorded: **10 January 1956, RCA Nashville**
First released: **27 January 1956, c/w I Was The One**

This was the one, the song that gave Elvis the world.

The story of Heartbreak Hotel's genesis begins in Gainsville, Florida. Local musician Tommy Durden noticed a story on the front page of the *Miami Herald*, with a picture of a suicide and the headline, 'Do you know this man?' Durden was struck by a detail in the story: that the anonymous corpse had only one thing on him, a note that read 'I walk a lonely street'.

He took that notion over to the house of a friend, Mae Axton, a 40-year-old schoolteacher and local TV personality who had worked as publicist on the Florida section of a 1955 Elvis tour, and who tried to be a songwriter but only had the one hit (though it was one that President Bill Clinton would later play sax to on Arsenio Hall's TV chat show). Her son Hoyt grew up to write both The Pusher for Steppenwolf and Never Been To Spain for Elvis.

Mae Axton knew that a single man in possession of a new recording contract must be in want of a hit song. So she sat Durden down, and together they wrote Heartbreak Hotel, then had it demoed by Glen Reeves, who spurned the offer of a slice of the royalties in lieu of payment. In What Was The First Rock'N'Roll Record? the authors report that Reeves' actual words were: 'That's the silliest song I ever heard.'

A few weeks later, Mae Axton played the Heartbreak Hotel demo to Elvis in Nashville. According to her, he liked it straightaway and said: 'Hot dog, Mae, play it again.' A couple of months after that, he took it to his first RCA recording session. He'd just turned 21.

The session kicked off with a regular from Elvis's stage show, Ray Charles' I've Got A Woman. Then RCA A&R man Steve Sholes turned the echo right up in an attempt to copy the unique 'slapback' sound Sam Phillips got at Sun. The musicians went straight into Heartbreak Hotel, Elvis pretty much copying Reeves' demo.

Steve Sholes didn't know it yet. In fact, he didn't like it very much. But he'd just made a hit record, Elvis' first. It was the seventh take of the second song.

Within two years, in Harper's Magazine, James and Annette Baxter would write: 'He went too far in every direction. Elvis was making millions of dollars, owning white Continental Mark IIs, getting into fights, reviving sideburns and building a house for his parents. The gawky, loose-limbed simple boy from Tupelo, Mississippi, was a genuine tabula rasa, on which the American public could keep drawing its portrait, real and imaginary, and keep rubbing it out.' *ep*

Blue Suede Shoes
Written by: **Carl Perkins**
Recorded: **30 January 1956, RCA, New York**
First released: **on Elvis Presley EP, March 1956**

Did Elvis ever own a pair of blue suede shoes? Not to anyone's knowledge. Though he did own pink jackets and peg trousers with zig-zags down the side seam, bought from Lansky Brothers, a store on Beale Street, the centre of black Memphis — where he would certainly have seen coloured suede shoes, which were a big mid-1950s fashion favourite of southern black pimps and those who would dress like them.

The name of the man who owned the footwear which inspired Blue Suede Shoes has never been established, but we do know he lived in Jackson, Tennessee and liked to dance. Which is why he was spotted by Carl Perkins, the song's writer and one of Elvis' fellow Sun recording artists. Playing a show at a Jackson honky tonk, Perkins noticed a young man who seemed less concerned with his dancing partner than in making sure his brand new shoes didn't get messed up. Then Perkins recalled a story told him by Johnny Cash (also a Sun artist at the time) about a black airforceman who'd tell people not to step on his 'blue suede shoes', a joking reference to his service boots. Perkins put the two stories together, kicked off with a line taken from a children's rhyme, and had himself a hit record.

It was released on 1 January 1956, backed by Honey Don't — which the Beatles later recorded with Ringo singing, as he did on two other Perkins' songs, Everybody's Trying To Be My Baby and Carl's rewrite of a very old Blues, Matchbox. It hit all three charts, selling as well to blacks as it did to whites. Unlike Elvis, though, Carl Perkins' chart career stopped there, halted by a car crash and the alcoholism from which he only emerged some years later.

Elvis' version of Blue Suede Shoes was recorded out of fear. Steve Sholes, who had signed Elvis to RCA, was worried that he'd made a mistake. Although they had cut what turned out to be Elvis' first big hit, Heartbreak Hotel, Sholes was wracked by doubt. So at Elvis' second session, Sholes did what every record company A&R man did in those days. He took a record that was just climbing the chart and got his artist to cover it.

Although Elvis was unhappy about copying a song by one of his former label's big hopes, he went along with Sholes. Out of thirteen takes, the tenth was chosen. It's probably better than Perkins' original, and certainly more of a Pop song, being less tied down by Perkins' Country roots. But it was only a minor hit in the US, in March that year, on Elvis' first EP. Though Elvis performed it several times on TV, he reportedly prevailed on Sholes not to release it as a single. He didn't want to spoil the chart chances of Perkins and Sam Phillips. Being Elvis, he also re-recorded it years later, for the movie GI Blues, as a piece of fluff. **ep**

(E is for Enquirer)

The *National Enquirer*, which printed a five-part version of the Elvis — What Happened? revelations and paid Elvis' cousin Bobby Mann $75,000 to take a secret photograph of Elvis in his coffin — though some say Elvis looks too young in it for it to be anything but a fake. It was published on the cover dated 6 September, 1977. The sales were a record-breaking 6.5 million. A year later, on 20 September, 1977, the Enquirer also published the final photograph of Elvis alive — taken on the eve of his death by a fan as he drove into Graceland at 12.28am.

My Baby Left Me
Written by: **Arthur Crudup**
Recorded: **30 January 1956, RCA New York**
Released: **c/w I Want You, I Need You, I Love You, May 1956**

The theme here is: you can take the boy out of Memphis, but you can't take Memphis out of the boy. On his second, post-Sun recording session — and his first in New York — Elvis recorded not one but two more songs by Arthur Big Boy Crudup, the Bluesman who had written his first single, That's All Right (Mama). My Baby Left Me was cut first, right after Blue Suede Shoes, and So Glad You're Mine was recorded later the same day.

Both are as close in sound and feel to the Sun sides as anything Elvis did after leaving the label. There are drums — which there weren't on That's All Right — and there is the acoustic clarity of the big New York studio. But otherwise this is just a big-city version of the rockabilly which Elvis, Scotty and Bill had been developing since they'd first cooked it up that July night eighteen months earlier. If anything, it's more Countrified than before. Elvis shouts 'Play the Blues, boy' to Scotty. And Scotty takes his solo, playing as Country as he ever did. (There's an odd link here — with Elvis' 1970s version of Reconsider Baby, where James Burton is also told by Elvis to 'play the blues' but instead takes a country solo.)

Although the stories that Elvis later paid for a Crudup recording session seem to be false, he does seem to have retained great affection for the man's songs. My Baby Left Me crops up again on 1974's As Recorded Live On Stage In Memphis album. *ep*

Lawdy Miss Clawdy
Written by: **Lloyd Price**
Recorded: **3 February 1956, RCA New York**
First released: **flip side of Shake, Rattle And Roll, September 1956**

On 19 November, 1955, Elvis flew to New York with his new manager, Colonel Parker, and signed to RCA Records. He stayed at the Warwick Hotel and was already famous enough to be inundated by phone calls and letters from young fans. But, according to Ted Fox in Showtime At The Apollo, he spent his nights alone, uptown in Harlem. That week, the show at the theatre on 125th Street featured the likes of Bo Diddley, Honky-Tonk pianist Bill Doggett, doo-woppers such as the Flamingoes and the Harptones, R&B boomer Etta James and former Sun recording artist, Howlin' Wolf. Fox imagines Elvis at the Apollo: 'even his perfectly sculpted, slicked-back pompadour, black pants and pink shirt did not set him apart. The look that had seemed so bizarre in hometown Memphis was de rigueur in Harlem.' It is unlikely he was recognised, though the Apollo patrons may well have heard his recent hit Mystery Train. 'But they probably thought Elvis Presley was a black man. He certainly sounded like one.'

In his early RCA days, Elvis sang a lot of other people's R&B, covering several recent and not so recent black hits, among them Little Richard's Tutti Frutti, Joe Turner's Shake, Rattle And Roll, Ray Charles' I've Got A Woman, the Drifters' Money Honey and, most dynamically of all, Lloyd Price's Lawdy Miss Clawdy. A number one R&B hit in 1952, it was recorded in New Orleans by Art Rupe, owner of the Hollywood-based R&B label, Speciality. Rupe went to New Orleans in search of the 'another Fats Domino' and found a 17-year-old, piano-playing airport worker. Lloyd Price took the song's title from the favourite phrase of local R&B dee-jay James 'Okie Dokie' Smith who'd shout 'Lawdy Miss Clawdy!' any time something pleased him.

Clearly a phonetic spelling of Lordy, the word 'Lawdy' first appeared on a record in 1929, on Blind Teddy Darby's Lawdy Lawdy Blues. In 1943 both Andy Kirk and Roy Milton cut Hey Lawdy Mama and in 1950 Jimmy Witherspoon recorded Miss Clawdy B. Just as clearly, the tune was definitely 'another Fats Domino', which was unsurprising since Domino's band play on it. Its more distant roots, though, are in the Havana of the 1920s — the origin of the three-note bass triad which so dominates Lawdy Miss Clawdy and many other New Orleans R&B hits of the 1950s. 'Son', they call it in Cuba, and claim it came from Africa, though there is no real proof.

Lawdy Miss Clawdy was one of the first black records to cross over. 'To my knowledge it was the first,' said Art Rupe. 'Why, I can't tell you. But white kids began to buy this record. They had heard it on black stations and I think it started in the south oddly enough, where we felt there was the most prejudice. Politically there was prejudice, but not musically.' *ep*

Hound Dog

Written by: **Jerry Leiber, Mike Stoller**
Recorded: **2 July 1956, RCA, New York**
First released: **c/w Don't Be Cruel, July 1956**

For a song that defines Elvis for so many people, Hound Dog has the oddest of histories, graced by a list of characters that would have fitted the bill for a follow-up to The Maltese Falcon: two Jewish teenagers from LA one of whose uncles answered to the name of Dave the Number 'King', Mike Stoller and Jerry Leiber, who originally wrote the song back in 1952 for ... a grossly overweight black lesbian Blues singer called Willie Mae Thornton (Big Mama to friends). She recorded it at Hollywood's Radio Recorders (the same studio Elvis would use to cut all his film soundtracks) backed by the band of ... a Greek drummer who pretended he was black — Johnny Otis, who then tried to steal a co-credit for Hound Dog when it was put out by ... a pale-skinned Irish-Jewish Negro gangster from Houston who was a Don — Don Robey, that is, owner of Peacock Records. When Hound Dog became a number one R&B hit, Robey was sued by ... an almost blind music business hustler from Cincinnati, name of Syd Nathan, who claimed he had Otis under exclusive contract. Robey meanwhile sued ... an Alabama farm boy turned Memphis record label owner called Sam Phillips, who had put out Bear Cat by Rufus Thomas, an 'answer record' to Hound Dog which blatantly contravened the original copyright and gave Sun Records its first hit in spring 1953. While it was still on the charts ... a strange-looking young man from the Memphis projects — with 'long, greasy, dirty-blond hair' — wandered into the Sun studio and told Sam's secretary, Marion Keisker, 'I sing all sorts.'

Elvis, though, found his Hound Dog in Las Vegas, where he played his first, terribly unsuccessful season in April 1956, on the back of Heartbreak Hotel. Big Mama Thornton's Hound Dog is a sloping, growling Blues, with lyrics obviously tailored for a fat black lesbian. Elvis' is a bright Pop song, a novelty record almost, with slightly different lyrics that don't quite make sense — how, for example, can a 'high-classed' dog be 'cryin' all the time'?

That lyrical twist and the new arrangement — including the earth-shattering drum pattern — were provided by a Las Vegas 'lounge act', Freddy Bell and the Bell Boys, whose show was a parody of early Rock'n'Roll bands. 'We stole it straight from them,' said Scotty Moore. Elvis introduced Hound Dog as the closing number of his own show, at the New Frontier Hotel. That is, he took to finishing his act with his version of what was effectively already someone else's parody of himself.

This was the period of national uproar about his stage movements, of Time magazine calling him Elvis The Pelvis. So, two months later, when he performed the song live on the Steve Allen

TV show, on 1 July in New York, he disarmed his critics by singing it to a Basset hound.

He recorded it the next morning, along with Don't Be Cruel and Anyway You Want Me. Much to everyone's surprise, this song that Elvis, Scotty and Bill had been performing live for nearly three months proved very hard to record. It wasn't until the thirty-first take that session overseer, RCA's Steve Sholes, called out 'Okay, Elvis. I think we've got it.'

A month later, at a press conference in Miami, Elvis was asked what he thought about an item that was dominating the news — an Italian cruise ship, the Andrea Doria, had sunk in the north Atlantic and survivors were making their way to New York. 'I haven't had time to read a newspaper,' said Elvis. 'And therefore I have no opinion.' At which, he broke up the press conference and, according to June Juanico's memoir of her time as Elvis' girlfriend, started shaking his head. Furious, he said: 'I should've asked that son of a bitch if he knew anything about rock'n'roll music. What kind of asshole would ask me a stupid question like that?'

Stupid or not, it was prescient — one of the Andrea Doria passengers was Hound Dog's writer Mike Stoller. 'I was sitting in a lifeboat with sixty or seventy other people, relieved to be away from the Andrea Doria which now had a large gaping hole in its side and was going down fast. The lifeboat had a broken rudder and could not be steered. I wondered what would happen to me next. Fifteen hours later, I stepped on to the dock in New York and was greeted by Jerry Leiber with, among other things, the news that Elvis had just recorded Hound Dog.'

Despite the fact that Leiber and Stoller went on to have a fruitful and lucrative working relationship with Elvis, neither has ever made a secret about their distaste for his version of Hound Dog. They thought it vulgar, a banal and Poppy perversion of what was meant to be an almost-serious song of threat for a singer Mike Stoller described as 'a powerful, powerful woman', with what 'looked like knife scars on her face'.

It is said that Big Mama herself thought Elvis had stolen the song from her and that she attacked him for 'exploiting black artists'. While the charge is both wrong and unfair, it is clear that she never got much of a crack at life. Hound Dog was her only hit and she eventually retired from show business — only to be rediscovered in the 1960s by white Texan caterwauler Janis Joplin who took Big Mama's Ball And Chain and tortured it to death on a million-selling album, the aptly titled Cheap Thrills. Big Mama died, broke and broken-spirited, in 1984.

By contrast, Leiber and Stoller never complained about Elvis' lyrical change to their song — which would have been their legal right as authors. That's what happens when a record sells seven million and becomes featured in the Elvis Presley lipstick range — Hound Dog Orange was the precise shade. *ep*

Don't Be Cruel

Written by: **Otis Blackwell, Elvis Presley**
Recorded: **2 July 1956, RCA New York**
First released: **c/w Hound Dog, July 1956**

In 1986, on the founding of the Rock'n'Roll Hall Of Fame, Rolling Stone magazine interviewed Sam Phillips. Journalist Elizabeth Kaye asked him when exactly did he realise how big Elvis would be?

'Not when I heard Heartbreak Hotel,' he replied. 'That was the worst record. I knew it when I heard Don't Be Cruel. I was driving back from the first vacation I'd had in my life and it came on the radio, and I said: "Wait a minute. Jesus, he's off and gone, man". I'd like to run off the road.'

Elizabeth Kaye then asked if that had made him jealous.

'Hell, no, because when I heard Heartbreak Hotel, I said: "Damned sons of bitches are going to mess this man up". Then, boy, I heard Don't Be Cruel and I was the happiest man in the world.'

Vernon Chadwick, an English professor at the University of Mississippi, concurs — at the 1996 Elvis conference, he claimed that Don't Be Cruel was to Elvis what the Sermon On The Mount was to Jesus.

Otis Blackwell wrote Don't Be Cruel — though that is not what it says on the label. To this day, the credit is joint, Blackwell-Presley, but that is simple theft. 'I was told that I would have to make a deal,' was Blackwell's calm explanation. He was a New York R&B singer who'd grown up on both Blues and Country music — 'a little coloured fellow in a derby hat' was the description given by Jerry Lee Lewis whose biggest hit, Great Balls Of Fire, was also written by Blackwell.

1956 was the start of a great run for Blackwell. Little Willie John had just had an enormous R&B hit with the original version of his song Fever. The following year it would hit the Pop charts, the year after that Peggy Lee would make it into an even bigger hit. In the future were more Elvis records — notably All Shook Up and Return To Sender — and the great Mod favourite, Daddy Rolling Stone.

Like nearly all those who provided songs for Elvis, Blackwell never met the man who made him rich. He cut the demo for Don't Be Cruel at Charlie Brave's Allegro studio in the basement of 1650 Broadway, New York. Elvis pretty much copied it — though it took twenty-eight takes to get there — using a a number of Blackwell's distinctive vocal twists and turns. Blackwell got touchy about Elvis' debt to his singing style over the years, feeling he'd never had quite the credit he was due. In 1978 he put out an album called These Are My Songs.

Don't Be Cruel became Elvis' biggest hit to date, topping not just the Pop and Country charts but also the R&B one. Elvis had, for a brief time, reunited black and white Pop musics — and their audiences. It was around this time that Elvis appeared at the Palace, the black theatre in downtown Memphis. Torn down in the devastating redevelopment of Beale Street in the 1960s, the Palace was at the junction of Beale and Hernando, a block down the hill from where a giant Elvis statue stood for some time in the 1980s.

Elvis wasn't there to sing, just to lend his face to a charity evening organised by WDIA, the local black radio station. Nat D Williams was there. Dee-jay, nationally-syndicated black journalist and teacher at Booker T Washington High School, where many of Stax records' future stars were then being educated, Mr Williams recorded what he saw in his column: 'A thousand black, brown, and beige teenage girls in that audience blended their alto and soprano voices in one wild crescendo of sound that rent the rafters, and took off like scalded cats in the direction of Elvis.' With Otis Blackwell's help, Elvis had become the biggest star on Beale Street, an awkward fact for those who would suggest his career was based on stealing from black musicians. *ep*

(F is for Fred)

My guide on the tour of the Sun Studios in Memphis. I took it on a bleak November morning and fortified myself for the trip with breakfast in the attached cafe, third booth from the window — which is where Sam Phillips used to conduct his business in the early days of Sun when it was known as Miss Taylor's Restaurant.

I ate — of course — a fried peanut butter and banana sandwich. Truly, 'a breakfast fit for a king'. (Anyone interested in repeating the experience in the privacy of their own home should consult one of the Elvis recipe books: Are You Hungry Tonight? by Brenda Arlene Butler, say, or Fit For A King by Elizabeth McKeon.)

I laughed as I ordered it from the waiter. He gave me a dishwater look. 'Do people always laugh when they order that breakfast?' I said. 'Yes,' he said, resignedly.

Because of the earliness of the hour and the chill of the day, I was the only one making the tour that hour. I had Fred all to myself. But he did the whole thing as if there were a big crowd of people there. He's an actor of sorts, I suppose. The story he tells is really a script he's learned. But he's learned it well and spoke it with surprising freshness.

It's a very good story, anyway, a well-constructed history — from Sam Phillips starting the label right through to U2 using the tiny studio to record When Love Comes To Town with BB King. Fred outlines the social background, tells you about the musicians, plays snatches of songs, shows you the instruments and the equipment used. It's literate, accurate — and honest. At one point, Fred stands in the corner by the door to the control room and grabs hold of a big old microphone, a great hunk of time-dulled stainless steel. You think: I know that microphone, I've seen it in pictures, it's the one Elvis used when he recorded at Sun. And Fred says: 'This is a microphone just like the one Elvis used when he recorded at Sun. Not the real one. But one just like it.' Thanks Fred.

All Shook Up
Written by: **Otis Blackwell**
Recorded: **12 January 1957, Radio Recorders, Hollywood**
First released: **c/w Teddy Bear, 6 April, 1957**

It is said that All Shook Up was inspired by Elvis' favourite drink, Pepsi Cola. If so, it's of a piece with this still-common English playground chant:

I went to a Chinese restaurant
To buy a loaf of bread, bread, bread.
They wrapped it up in a £5 note
And this is what they said, said, said:
'My name is Elvis Presley.
Girls are sexy, sitting in
The back seat drinking Pepsi.'
They go kiss, kiss,
We go: 'Wow ...'

   Like Don't Be Cruel, it was written by Otis Blackwell — the previous day, according to some accounts. The credit, untruthfully, claims Elvis as a co-writer. But he does play guitar on it. And he keeps a straight face singing what is an odd line even by the standards of 1950s Pop — 'I'm itching like a man in a fuzzy tree'. *ep*

Peace In The Valley
Written by: **Thomas A Dorsey**
Recorded: **13 January 1957, Radio Recorders**
First released: **on Peace In The Valley EP, April 1957**

Sincerity is too refined and focused a word to use when examining something as floppy as Elvis' religious beliefs. There is no doubt he thought of himself as a religious, even spiritual man. He grew up dreaming of being — sometimes simultaneously, sometimes alternately — both a great Pop singer and a great Gospel singer. Like that other rocker Jerry Lee Lewis, he apostrophised his body and soul as the Lord's battleground, seeing vast, dramatic struggles sweeping across him — sometimes victory went to God, sometimes to the other guy.

Often, he seemed to see all religion as little more than an extension of himself. His reading of the Bible included the revelations that because he was rich he was going to heaven and that it was okay for him to be sexually promiscuous because Jesus also slept with the women who followed him. This did not endear him to Priscilla. Nor did the Bible-reading classes he'd lead in their LA home, since most of the fellow readers tended to be young women wearing far too few clothes for their own good. He also read Kahlil Gibran's The Prophet rather a lot. 'He flapped in the wind of his passions,' wrote Van K Brock.

Elvis' gospel recordings were the arena in which these patchwork-quilt beliefs were demonstrated, if not worked out. Like so much of American music at this time, Peace In The Valley was a piece of miscegenation worthy of Elvis' own racial and spiritual confusions. Most of Elvis' audience would probably have known the song as a 1951 hit for Country singer Red Foley — who also performed the original version of Old Shep, the first song Elvis sang in public and which he'd recorded three months earlier.

But it was written many years earlier by a black Georgian who was as torn between sin and salvation as Elvis. In the Devil's corner, he was Georgia Tom, writing Blues of incomparable filth such as It's Tight Like That. On the Lord's side, he was Thomas A Dorsey whose tunes pretty much created what we know as black Gospel music — spirituals they called them back then; Gospel was the white Pentecostal singing Elvis took in with his mother's milk. Dorsey was saved for the Lord by the Reverend Nix's Black Diamond Express To Hell sermon, 'with Sin the Engineer, holding the throttle open; Pleasure is the Headlight, and the Devil is the Conductor.'

Dorsey himself uncrossed the contradiction in his heart thus: 'I always had rhythm in my bones. I like the solid beat. I like the long, moaning, groaning tone. I like the rock.'

Elvis' first public performance of Peace In The Valley was a week before the recording session, on The Ed Sullivan Show. This was the highwater mark of anti-Elvis fury in America. Such were the worries about his 'suggestive' hip movements that he was shot only from the waist up. It is not being too cynical, therefore, to suggest that choosing this moment to start recording Gospel was not the daftest of career moves. What better way to demonstrate 'wholesomeness' to the great mass of Americans?

That Elvis — and the Colonel — had no intention of forgetting the secular is shown by the other songs recorded that day, which included All Shook Up and Mean Woman Blues; also by song credits for His Hand On Mine, the album on which it eventually appeared. Elvis copped the credit, and therefore the money, for five 'traditional' songs on it, including something called 'Swing Down Sweet Chariot' — i.e. the aged spiritual, Swing Low Sweet Chariot.

That praising the Lord through song meant a great deal to Elvis, is not in doubt. Peace In The Valley is given a touchingly simple and unadorned reading, with an equal balance between his voice and those of the Jordanaires. He was forever telling anyone who listened that he wanted his voice lower on the mix of his records so that they sounded more like the singing of the Blackwood Brothers the Gospel quartet he so loved as a teenager.

Elvis was nominated for fourteen Grammys, but only won three, all of them for Gospel material. I suspect he'd have considered this a sign from the Lord.

In 1992, a book entitled Elvis People — The Cult Of The King by Ted Harrison, a respected theological writer, was published in England. 'Over the centuries,' he wrote, 'many cults and religions have been started. The Elvis cult is one of the latest.' What would Elvis himself have made of that? I suspect he'd have thought that a sign from the Lord, too. **ep**

(Let Me Be Your) Teddy Bear
Written by: **Kal Mann, Bernie Lowe**
Recorded: **24 January 1957, Radio Recorders, Hollywood**
First released: **c/w Loving You, June 1957**

Teddy Bear is a real Tin Pan Alley song with some terrible lyrics. 'Lions are not the ones that love enough' — what on earth does that mean? But somehow the basic conceit transcends the base cynicism with which it was written.

If anything, that cynicism was exceeded by the marketing of the song. It's mostly been stated that a month before recording Teddy Bear, Elvis received 282 stuffed bears as spontaneous Christmas gifts from fans. The truth is that Colonel Parker, knowing Elvis was to cut Teddy Bear, put about the lie that Elvis collected teddy bears. Fans took it seriously and Elvis got landed with truckloads of stuffed bears, which he promptly re-routed to the National Foundation for Infantile Paralysis.

The single itself — like Jailhouse Rock and Don't Be Cruel — was a number one hit on all three charts — Pop, R&B and Country. Later Elvis tried to unite his nation with An American Trilogy, bringing black and white, north and south back together through song. But he did it first with a little stuffed animal. *ep*

(G is for Gates)

Bill, owner of Microsoft — who posted this e-mail communication at www.elvissightings.com on Monday, 24 February, 1997 at 13:00:40 (EST) — Bgates@microsoft.com Elvis was never alive, he was a computer-generated figure, and his voice was the work of Creative labs. In 1977 Microsoft decided to put all of our focus on Windows, and the Elvis project was dropped. Sorry.

(Let Me Be Your) Teddy Bear

When It Rains, It Really Pours
Written by: **William Robert Emerson**
Recorded: **24 February 1957, Radio Recorders**
First released: **on Elvis For Everyone LP, 1965**

This was, in fact, the second time Elvis had cut a version of When It Rains, It Really Pours. The first attempt, which didn't appear for nearly thirty years, till 1983's Elvis — A Legendary Performer Vol 4, was the last track Elvis cut for Sun before leaving for RCA Records. That session was a failure but even so it's clear that the song itself is a strong and idiosyncratic Blues, with a fabulously impenetrable phrase: 'She really opened up my nose.' It's said that it was one of Elvis' favourite songs of 1954. But the most likely reason Sam Phillips chose it was that he owned the copyright: it was written by Sun artist Billy 'The Kid' Emerson and recorded a few months after Elvis' That's All Right (Mama). It was one of the last Blues sides that Sam Phillips cut.

Emerson was a member of Ike Turner's Kings Of Rhythm band and it was Ike who brought him to Sun. When It Rains was his best-selling single, though he was convinced that Sam was more interested in Elvis covering it. 'He wanted Elvis to cut it as a single,' said Emerson. 'Elvis himself, he was a real sweet kid. The white guys didn't talk to us coloured guys too much back then, but Elvis was different.'

Emerson's original version is dominated by a honking sax. Elvis' Hollywood version is graced by battering drums and a Scotty Moore guitar solo which is part jazz, part simple spanking — his reference, I imagine, to the sax on Emerson's. The very noisiness of it is probably the reason it wasn't released for eight years. It finally came out on 1965's Elvis For Everyone album which contained the strangest mixture of songs, even by the standards of a mid-1960s Elvis album. There was everything from Italo-schmaltz, Santa Lucia, to Hank Williams' Your Cheatin' Heart, to the first, string-enhanced appearance of Tomorrow Night, one of Elvis' very first Sun recordings. At his best, Elvis could bring together the most disparate of sources and make them one.

Not on Elvis For Everyone, he couldn't.

Jailhouse Rock

Written by: **Jerry Leiber, Mike Stoller**
Recorded: **30 April 1957, Radio Recorders**
First released: **c/w Treat Me Nice, September 1957**

The theme is the male homosexual experience in the US prison system. The text is the second verse of Jailhouse Rock: inmate number 47 informs inmate number 3 that he is the 'cutest jailbird' he's ever seen and looks forward to spending time in his 'company', adding that this should take the form of doing the 'jailhouse rock'. And the question is: are we talking consenting adults here or male rape?

Jailhouse Rock was written for Elvis' third movie by Jerry Leiber and Mike Stoller. 'Ambiguity is a big part of Jerry's work,' said Stoller.

Although Elvis had already recorded four of their songs, this was the first time they had worked with him in the studio, the start of the most important working relationship of Elvis' recording career in the late 1950s. Effectively commissioned to write the Jailhouse Rock soundtrack, by Jean Aberbach of Elvis' publishers, Hill & Range, they weren't overjoyed at the prospect. They considered themselves to be young hipsters and they'd really loathed what he'd done to Hound Dog. As Mike Stoller explained to Elvis biographer Peter Guralnick in Last Train To Memphis: 'We thought we were the only two white kids who knew anything about the Blues.' Which leads to the thought that they put the homosexual theme in Jailhouse Rock as a deliberate, considered way to tease someone who they, as sophisticated Hollywood hipsters, reckoned was a southern hick who wouldn't get the joke.

The Jailhouse Rock recording session was the first time Leiber and Stoller met Elvis, in fact. This is the way Leiber tells it: 'We thought he was like an idiot savant but he listened a lot. He knew all of our records. He knew Eddie 'Cleanhead' Vinson. He loved Ray Charles' early records. And he was a workhorse in the studio — he didn't pull any diva numbers.'

And this is the way Stoller tells it: 'At first we just talked generally about music and making records, then we drifted over to the piano and got to know each other better. Elvis and I played some four-hand blues for a while before we settled down to business. I sat at the piano and Jerry kicked off a run-through of Jailhouse Rock. It was starting to feel good. Jerry made some suggestions to DJ [Fontana, the drummer] and Bill [Black, the bassist] and we tried it again. It was great. Elvis said: okay, let's make it. Jerry ran into the control booth and set the tempo, snapping his fingers over the intercom. And that is the way those sessions went — with Jerry directing from inside the booth, me at the piano and everyone else doing what they knew how to do. Sometimes we would get a tune in one or two takes. Sometimes we did as many as twenty five.'

For the record, Jailhouse Rock took six — both for the single hit version and the one used in the movie, which just has a few extra overdubs. The scene featuring it is the finest couple of minutes of Elvis' entire cinematic career. Elvis is the jailed singing truck-driver Vince Everett. Dressed in the coolest white-stitched denim prison uniform you've ever seen, he performs in the centre of a grid of cells, surrounded by a dozen first-rate dancers playing his fellow inmates. The choreographer, who based the dance on Elvis' own movements, helps create a moment which is both a camp classic and far, far sexier than any of Elvis' movie love scenes with beautiful women.

Which leaves one question: if Elvis wasn't in on the joke, who the hell did he think he was singing to? And one quote, from DJ Fontana on his drum part: 'I tried to think of someone on a chain gang smashing rocks.' *ep*

Don't

Written by: **Jerry Leiber, Mike Stoller**
Recorded: **6 September 1957, Radio Recorders**
First released: **c/w I Beg Of You, January 1958**

Don't, Leiber and Stoller's second successive number one hit for Elvis, prefigures the late, fat Elvis more than anything else he recorded till the early 1960s. It's overblown and grandiose. He uses his deep, operatic voice for the first time. And it steps along at a pace more often heard in martial music.

That it somehow makes sense of itself is quite probably because of its duplicity. Like so many Leiber and Stoller songs, it is not quite what it seems on first hearing; its stentorian tone conceals a libertine's narrative. Basically, it is a song of seduction — don't say don't — masquerading as a lover's innocent plea. Elvis makes the song work because he treats both readings — the one on the surface and the double entendre — as equally plausible.

He's able to do that because it's a reflection of the private Elvis. As evidence I quote from Elvis: In The Twilight Of Memory by June Juanico who dated him right through the summer of 1956. It is morning, Elvis and June have slept the night together in a hotel bed, without having sex. His parents are in the next room. June writes: 'I raised my hips, making it easy for him to remove my borrowed briefs. Evidently he was feeling the same way as me. All the other times when we'd been in this situation I had stopped him, or he had stopped himself, saying he wanted it to be special. He said he wanted to wait until we were married. So did I, but this time our passion for each other had taken us too far, pushed us both out of control. We had made love, in our own special way, every time we were together, but this was the first time we actually came close to physically having sex. Elvis was slowly and gently beginning to enter me when we heard a tap-tap-tap at the door.' It is Elvis' mother, Gladys, suggesting contraception.

Don't was the first song Leiber and Stoller wrote for Elvis at his instigation: he asked Mike Stoller to write 'a real pretty ballad' for him. It was also the beginning of the end for Leiber and Stoller's brief close working relationship with him — for a good part of 1957 and 1958, Leiber and Stoller were the closest thing to a regular producer that Elvis had in his entire recording career. Both the Colonel and Elvis' song-publishing company hated this relationship. Simply, it threatened their power over Elvis. Leiber and Stoller wrote Don't over a weekend, cutting a demo of it with Young Jessie, an R&B singer who worked with them as a member of the Coasters. On Monday, they played it to Elvis. He smiled and said, 'That's real pretty, that's just what I wanted.' Three months later he cut it, along with Blue Christmas, some vaguely religious seasonal stuff and Santa Claus Is Back in Town, the sleaziest double entendre that Leiber and Stoller ever wrote — or that Elvis ever recorded. *ep*

(H is for Harrelson)

Woody, actor and Elvis fan whose life story sounds like it just climbed out of a Jerry Lee Lewis song. It's possible that there is very little character acting in his portrayals of a (very) simple country boy in the TV sitcom Cheers and a sleaze-pit of a pornographer in The People Vs Larry Flynt. The son of a Texan good ol' boy turned contract killer — who got two life sentences in 1979 — and a bible-bashing Presbyterian mother, his first acting role was the Elvis impression he used to impress his classmates at school. Like Jerry Lee himself, he went on to study theology and chase women. At one time, he reckoned he was racking up three women a day. 'I was like a kid in a candy store.' Like Elvis he has now found solace in the spiritual, doing yoga eight hours a day.

Another actor, Eddie Murphy, is an even bigger Elvis fan, has pictures of him on his walls. But, for an obvious reason, it's unlikely he'll be playing Elvis in any biopic. Mr Murphy is from New York, you see.

Elvis Alphabet

Santa Claus Is Back In Town
Written by: **Jerry Leiber, Mike Stoller**
Recorded: **7 September 1957**
First released: **on Elvis' Christmas Album and Elvis Sings Christmas Songs EP, December 1957**

To say that Santa Claus Is Back In Town is not a run-of-the-mill Yuletide celebration is something of an understatement. Between them, Elvis and the writers — Leiber and Stoller — achieve the seemingly impossible balance of creating a track that is simultaneously a Christmas love song and stunningly raucous and dirty. A slurring, backroom Blues riff that could double as a stripper's soundtrack is set against an angelic choir and Elvis at his sleaziest, singing words smutty enough for Mae West to later record her own version of it.

It was written in the studio, towards the end of the sessions for Elvis' Christmas Album. There wasn't enough material to fill it so Leiber and Stoller went off into a side room and wrote it, in fifteen minutes. It sounds like it too. Not because it's not good but because the discipline of time meant that for once, Leiber and Stoller couldn't demonstrate the full extent of their intelligence. Unlike all their other blues songs, this one is a bit dumb, pleasantly so — simple, in both meanings of the word.

It's a first-person narrative, with Santa Claus as the persona, and features some novel developments in the jolly old gent's lifestyle. Since 1821, when the fact was established in a poem published by New York printer William Gilley, Santa Claus' chosen means of transport had always been reindeer-powered sled. (The full set of eight reindeer — Dasher, Dancer, Prancer, etc — came along a year later, in A Visit From St Nicholas by Clement Clarke Moore.) Leiber and Stoller's Santa, though, has entered the modern world, dumping both the traditional sack and the 'sleigh with reindeer' in favour of 'a big black Cadillac'.

As Jailhouse Rock shows, Leiber and Stoller were masters of the sly double entendre. In the second verse of Santa Claus they display their gift for the schoolyard double entendre. Elvis as Santa suggests that the listener hang up their 'pretty stockings', turn off the light and prepare themselves for a visitation from Santa Claus who will be 'coming down' their chimney that very night.

The oddest thing is that when the Elvis Christmas album came out, religious fundamentalists complained not about this track but about the version of White Christmas — which was pretty much a copy of the (black) Drifters' 1954 R&B hit. Presumably they were concerned that it committed sacrilege against the Bing Crosby original. *ep*

Elvis' Farewell To His Fans

Recorded: **22 September 1958**
First released: **on Elvis Sails EP, December 1958**

This is a record of a moment of great symbolic importance in the Elvis mystery play. In The Hitchiker's Guide To Elvis, Mick Farren expresses himself with the true fury of a fan of the young Hillbilly Cat Elvis: 'The bastards were dragging Elvis off to the Army. We knew there was no point in pretending, the drafting of Elvis wasn't just something that happened. It was an ancient and evil ritual. They weren't merely giving Elvis an Army fresh-fish haircut; metaphysically, they were cutting his balls off. The fearful elders were castrating the Boy King, and we were all expected to watch.'

So what do we actually hear on the recording, first issued a couple of months later, on an EP which also featured a brief Christmas message to his fans? We hear the 'edited highlights' of an hour-long press conference, at which Elvis doesn't sound so much castrated as depressed at the thought of leaving the only country he'd ever understand and still wracked with grief at the death of his mother Gladys, a month earlier.

It's tempting to suggest he sensed in her death the black chill of his own future shadow passing over him. She'd treated him as an uncrowned prince all his life — they shared a bed until he was 13 — and she'd known, just known, that he'd be an important man one day. Then when that dream came true, she felt nothing but the hollowness of success: she'd gained a star but lost a son.

As Elvis would fifteen years later, she tried to fill that big aching hole with food, pills and vodka. A thin-faced countrywoman in her early life, she ballooned to freak-show size in her last years. Officially, she died of a heart attack after a bout of some kind of hepatitis — though as Elvis wouldn't give permission for an autopsy, it could well have been liver damage by the drink and drugs. She was 46 when she died, and looked 60.

The press conference was held at the Brooklyn Army Terminal in New York. The Colonel was there, of course. So were top executives from Hill & Range and RCA Records, several of Elvis' family, most of his pals and 125 newsmen. Holding a book of verse given to him by a soldier friend, Poems That Touch The Heart, Elvis answered the questions politely but distractedly. Wherever he was, it wasn't Brooklyn.

'I know you're a pretty tired fellow,' says a reporter, then adds with cherishable banality: 'How long, for example, has it been since you had a chance to eat today?'

'I had breakfast this morning,' Elvis replies. 'And I ain't had nothing to eat since then.'

To which the journalist responds with what should be, but probably isn't, fake astonishment. 'It's now two o'clock in the afternoon,' he says, seemingly devastated at the torture the day is

bringing to Elvis — who cuts back in with supplementary information: 'I don't feel I could eat anything right now.'

The questioning moves on to Elvis' imminent departure. 'I'm going to be very honest about it,' he says. 'I'm looking forward to Germany and meeting people. But at the same time I'm looking forward to coming back here.'

Finally he is asked if he has a message for his fans. He has. 'In spite of the fact that I'll be out of their eyes for some time, I hope I'm not out of their minds. I'd like to come back and entertain like I did and ...' At which point his voice trails away. He sounds like a man on Death Row.

The track finishes with Elvis leaving to board the USS Randolph and the sound of a slow, mournful ship's horn. In reality, as Elvis headed up the gangplank, a navy band played Tutti Frutti — eight times in all. They kept on repeating the scene until all the news and TV cameramen were happy with the result.

It is said that the Wall Street crash of 1929 marked the moment that New York became the capital of the world — the fact that the crash imploded every other economy proved it. The seriousness with which Elvis' departure to Germany was treated does something similar — this was the moment he became the world star of the twentieth century. *ep*

A Mess Of Blues
Written by: **Doc Pomus, Mort Shuman**
Recorded: **21 March 1960, RCA Nashville**
First released: **flip of It's Now Or Never, July 1960**

Elvis had just spent two years away with the army in Germany — being the perfect soldier, according to the press reports of the time; whooping it up with chorus lines of Parisian showgirls, according to the Goldman biography. He was back in the studio within two weeks of his discharge, his heels most likely sped by what turned out to be a groundless fear that his fans had lost interest while he was away. As it turned out, the already-titled Elvis Is Back racked up a million orders — 1,275,077, to be precise — even before he started recording it.

On sale within weeks, it was his first stereo album and the first which wasn't just a collection cobbled together from previous releases and odds and sods. It was also the first time Elvis recorded a song by Doc Pomus and Mort Shuman, the songwriting team whose work would be so important in re-establishing his career in the early 1960s.

Like Leiber and Stoller before them, Pomus and Shuman were a couple of big city white boys who fell for the Blues. Jerome E Felder 'Doc' Pomus, born in 1925, was the older of the pair by ten years. He'd written hits for Joe Turner (Still In Love), Ray Charles (Lonely Avenue) and the Coasters (Young Blood) when he joined up with Mort Shuman in 1958. They signed with Hill & Range — Elvis' publishers — and started writing little teenage blues ballads. Dion and the Belmonts' Teenager In Love and the Drifters' Save The Last Dance For Me were the biggies.

Later, when the Beatles came along, they moved to England. Pomus injured his back which put him in a wheelchair for life; after a fifteen-year break he took up songwriting again, with two notorious junkies — Dr John in the late-1970s and Mink DeVille in the early-1980s. He died in 1991. Shuman, meanwhile, wrote a string of hits including the Small Faces' Sha La La La Lee, with black popster turned golfer Kenny Lynch. Back in New York, he worked with Jerry Ragavoy on Howard Tate's great series of soul singles — including Get It While You Can and Look At Granny Run Run.

On his return to Europe, Shuman settled in Paris, working with France's only rock'n'roll star, Johnny Hallyday, then writing and starring in his own stage show, Jacques Brel Is Alive And Well And Living In Paris. Three years before his death in London, in 1991, he wrote Budgie, a musical, for Adam Faith. Oh yes, he worked with all the greats.

But the Elvis years were the glory years for the Pomus/Shuman partnership. On the surface, it would be easy to see them as successors to Leiber and Stoller in the Elvis music production line. But that would exaggerate their closeness to the operation. In fact, while

Leiber and Stoller were very much Elvis' producers for a short period, Pomus and Shuman were never more than his songwriters of choice for a few years. The general assumption is that when Leiber and Stoller started getting close to Elvis, Colonel Parker became so anxious about his position that he first eased them away, then ensured no one would ever again have such a close musical relationship with his client. Certainly neither Pomus nor Shuman, despite writing fifteen songs for Elvis, were ever allowed to meet him.

Elvis fans who write books about him tend to the belief that Elvis went 'soft' after the army. Which leaves the Pomus/Shuman songs wildly ignored, often in favour of the 'real Blues' he cut around the time — Reconsider Baby, say, and Feel So Bad. At best, the Pomus/Shuman songs are condescended to as 'classic Pop'. In fact, they are something far cleverer than that — they're a kind of missing link between the Broadway show tune and the Chicago blues. In an unassuming, unself-conscious way, they do what George Gershwin tried to do — somewhat patronisingly — with Rhapsody In Blue.

The show tune and the Bues stand in philosophical opposition to each other. It's not a matter of black versus white — there have always been plenty of sophisticated black American musicians and crude, amateurish white ones. It's more a question of sense versus sensibility. The Blues has the feeling while the show tune has the lyrical wit. Of course, there have always been uptown, Broadway versions of the Blues but they've nearly always been written by lyricists with tin ears. Consider the first-ever recorded Blues. It was written by a white minstrel from Dallas, sung by a white lawyer and businessman from Washington, George O'Connor, and called Nigger Blues.

The best Pomus/Shuman tunes, though, are genuinely sophisticated Blues Pop — even more so than Leiber and Stoller's. They combine the emotions and rhythmic feel of Blues with the structure and lyrical coherence of a Broadway show tune. While Leiber and Stoller's Pop Blues were mostly at their best when they were at their funniest — all the Coasters stuff, Santa Claus Is Back In Town and Jailhouse Rock for Elvis — Pomus/Shuman songs were rarely tongue in cheek. They were a unique mix — genuinely bluesy and genuinely teenage.

A Mess Of The Blues is one of the best and the most obviously bluesy, taking full advantage of both Elvis' ability to slur like a real bluesman and the professional session-man confidence of the Nashville studio band. There is nothing at all fake about it, none of the stupidity which infected so much 1950s pop music — from Elvis' dumb false start on Milkcow Blues Boogie to virtually every rockabilly track ever recorded. No-one here is trying to ingratiate themselves with the listener. The lyrical conceit — that of escape by train being a sensible, adult solution to heartbreak — is a Blues classic bordering on cliché. But the whole thing has such panache that familiarity adds rather than detracts from its impact. It has flair and wit, it swings, the drummer sounds like he's falling asleep and the finger-clicking (the singer's, I assume) is in perfect time, on the offbeat.

Strangely, it's probably one of the best-known of all Elvis tracks — not for itself but because it was the flip of another song cut at the same session, the 23 million-selling single, It's Now Or Never. *ep*

(I is for the first person singular)

and suggests two questions. One: like all Mama's boys and all pop stars, Elvis was strikingly self-centred, but exactly how self-centred was he? Two: is there an objective psychometric tool that could be used to measure this?

There is: take the total number of songs recorded and divide it by the sum of titles including a first person singular pronoun (ignoring anything within brackets) and express the result as a percentage. This is known as the Solipsism Index™.

Thus: according to The Elvis Encyclopaedia, he recorded 657 different songs. Of these, sixty one start with the first person singular and thirty more include it somewhere else in the title. A further eighty feature the first person accusative, genitive and dative. This gives a total of 171. (Five songs, by the way, include more than one first-person word. One features 'me' twice.) Performing the psychometric analysis on this data gives a figure of 26 per cent. Thus, Elvis' Solipsism Index™ is 0.26. In other words, Elvis was just over one quarter self-centred. By comparison, Frank Sinatra's Solipsism Index™ is 0.28.

The Girl Of My Best Friend

Written by: **Beverly Ross, Sam Bobrick**
Recorded: **4 April 1960, RCA Studio B, Nashville**
First released: **on Elvis Is Back LP, 1960**

Like (Marie's The Name Of) His Latest Flame, The Girl Of My Best Friend is almost a companion piece to Elvis' very first amateur recording, That's When Your Heartaches Begin. That was the story of best pal stealing best babe. As you'd expect from the title, The Girl Of My Best Friend flips the story. Set to a then-fashionable Latin rhythm, it's a genuinely sexy Pop song that, strangely, was only used as an album track. Elvis soundalike Ral Donner — who later narrated the 1986 movie This Is Elvis — took advantage of this, covered it and had a 1961 hit with it in the US, peaking at number 19. In the UK, by contrast it was a hit both straightaway, as the flipside of A Mess Of Blues, and again six months before Elvis died. *ep*

(J is for June Juanico)

The night before I met June Juanico, the woman Elvis Presley nearly married, I got talking to a man named Bayard in a bar in Oxford, Mississippi. A student at the university, born to wealth in Memphis, Bayard told me his aunt had dated Elvis. Doubtful, I asked him for how long. 'One night,' he said. Why only one night? 'She didn't enjoy the experience.' Why? 'White trash,' said Bayard.

I repeated this exchange to June over coffee at the Casino restaurant in Biloxi on Mississippi's Gulf Coast, where she meets and greets. 'He was not,' she said, then told me that when people find out she dated Elvis — for most of 1956 — they mostly ask her two questions: Can I touch you? and Did you sleep with Elvis? 'I tell 'em: yes to the first, no to the second,' said June. Those who read her sweet memoir Elvis: In The Twilight Of Memory will discover that her answer to the second question is both disingenuous and dependent on a definition of 'sleep with' as synonymous only with 'have full penetrative sex with'.

Such A Night

Written by: **Lincoln Chase**
Recorded: **4 April 1960, RCA Studio B, Nashville**
First released: **c/w Never Ending, July 1964**

If the accepted early take on Elvis had it that he was sex-on-legs, and far too filthy for his own good, the theory that developed over the years was Elvis as whitewasher, a larcenist of black material which he'd take and strip of its 'guts', 'soul' and 'sexuality' — for profit, glory and fame. Goldman based his entire Elvis aesthetic on that belief. The trouble is that it's just that: a belief, not a fact. Elvis' Such A Night could be used to justify a reverse thesis — that he made explicit what was only implicit in the R&B original.

Elvis shouts, whispers, screams, pleads, tries on different voices, swoops up and down the register — melisma, musicologists call it, it's a main calling card of the Blues. Fortunately the song can stand this robust treatment. It's a memoir of an ecstatic sexual encounter but one quite lacking the guilt and regret of, say, One Night which Elvis had recorded three years before, pre-army. This is post-army. It's clear Elvis learnt something in Germany, or on those showgirl-filled nights in Paris. This is certainly the only time Elvis sang about being 'filled with desire' and shared his memories of carousing till dawn. (Okay, I know the lyrics only refer to 'kissing' but, come on, we're all adults round here.)

And there's more. By the time he and the Jordanaires (male harmony group, remember) get to trading nonsense sounds (oohs, and ahs mostly), it sounds like nothing less than — and there is just no way to put this delicately — Elvis is having sex with all four of them simultaneously. And listen to how the song ends. First, the woman of memory disappears at dawn, then the memoirist sings: 'But before that dawn, ooh, aah, such a night!' What is that, but Elvis inviting us into his fantasy life, the orgasmic finale to a wet dream of a song?

While the sexual innuendo is there in the original version of Such A Night, it's of surprising delicacy. It was a 1954 hit, on the R&B charts only, for Clyde McPhatter and the Drifters. Like Elvis, McPhatter claimed Scottish ancestry. Unlike Elvis, though, he was black, one of the first R&B singers to spread the gospel from the church into the Pop charts. His singing on The Bells, a song of grief and loss recorded with Billy Ward and the Dominoes, makes Elvis' Such A Night sound like a selection from Hymns Ancient and Modern as performed at a suffocatingly proper English suburban parish church.

But on Such A Night, possibly because of the obviousness of the material, McPhatter is sweet and light. Above a trilling piano he sings it with perfect politeness. It sounds more like the Ink Spots than the other songs McPhatter was cutting with the Drifters at the time, Money Honey and a doo wop version of White Christmas. Elvis copied both well, too.

Johnnie Ray's 1954 Pop hit version of Such A Night is even less explicit — though that didn't stop both American radio stations and the BBC from banning it. They weren't stupid. They reckoned they knew what it was really about it. And they were right, as Elvis made so very clear six years later, in a Nashville recording studio.

Which is maybe why RCA didn't release it for another four years. By which time the world had changed, the pill had become available and the US had been swept up by the Beatles and their version of R&B history — while Elvis' reputation, understandably, given most of what he was doing, had fetched up on the dustheap of history. Fashion had moved on and it was barely noticed that very few Beatles R&B covers could stand comparison with the likes of Such A Night. Just as the Beatles started their run of US chart-topping singles, Such A Night levelled out at 16. ☞

Reconsider Baby
Written by: **Lowell Fulson**
Recorded: 4 **April 1960, RCA Nashville**
First released: **on Elvis Is Back LP, 1960**

Reconsider Baby was cut at Elvis' second set of post-Army sessions, a couple of weeks after the first — which had produced the first of that year's hit singles, Stuck On You, a couple of b-sides and a trio of album tracks. Albert Goldman, in his 1981 Elvis biography, makes some rather odd comments about Elvis' new appearance — 'very delicate and vulnerable', 'limp wrist, girlish grin and wobbly knees', 'he now looks outrageously gay'. However diligent his research usually was, Goldman clearly never listened to Reconsider Baby.

It's a big, swaggering blues song about adult heterosexual stuff — sex, love and desperation. Lowell Fulson who wrote it and had the first hit with it on Chess in 1954, was a black Okie who had his first successes in Texas, and wrote two of BB King's most famous tunes, Three O'Clock Blues and Everyday I Have The Blues. His version of Reconsider Baby — a plea to a departing lover, which stands no chance of success — is as urbane as guitar Blues gets. It has a great, lazy swing to it and Fulson's singing is unusually clear and unslurred for an R&B track. The piano clanks away, a small horn session sways moodily deep in the mix and Fulson's guitar notes arrive in thick, muddy-sounding handfuls. His solo is very similar to the stuff BB King was playing at the time — part T Bone Walker, part Charlie Christian. This was music for grown-up Blues fans — Saturday night close-dancing music for Southern blacks moved north.

Elvis' version inverts the Fulson arrangement. The original begins with Fulson's electric guitar echoed by the junkie-cool horn section. Elvis puts a sax where the guitar was and his own acoustic rhythm guitar where the horns were.

It was the last song recorded at the two-day-long session, which had already produced not only all the remaining tracks for his next album, Elvis Is Back, but also what would be his next two hit singles — It's Now Or Never and Are You Lonesome Tonight?. The band used on it was the same mix of old and new Elvis hands that worked on the March sessions. The Jordanaires were there, of course. Scotty Moore was on guitar as ever, joined by those other two long-time regulars, pianist Floyd Cramer and drummer DJ Fontana. But original bassist Bill Black was missing. When Elvis went into the army, Black built a career of his own — which he refused to abandon when Elvis returned. He was replaced by a couple of Nashville session musicians and an extra drummer was added — presumably the one who hits so hard on Reconsider Baby. The only new addition for the April sessions was sax player Boots Randolph.

Having worked all night, Elvis got to Reconsider Baby long after dawn — the studio musicians were moaning about not having enough time to shower before their next sessions, at ten o'clock that morning. Elvis sketches out the intro on his acoustic guitar, Boots Randolph joins in and they're off, making some of the best, sexiest music ever.

Bill Porter was the engineer. 'The mix is pretty hot,' he told Peter Guralnick. 'And there's a little distortion on the sax — I mean, there was nowhere to put it [in the mix]. Two takes, and that was it. We finished up about 7.15, 7.20am, played the tunes back, and then they split.'

Oddly, knowing just how puerile Elvis' own personal life was at this point — chasing an under-age virgin towards marriage while spending his Hollywood nights enticing pairs of 'actresses' to enact his lesbian fight

fantasies — doesn't detract at all from its impact. Rather, you just accept that he is mature only in his art. Hearing it, you forget what Goldman has told you about the real Elvis' love life; instead you listen to the musical Elvis' love life; you believe, without question, that he knows — and means — what he's singing about. You don't even think he's making a fool of himself when he shouts 'Play the blues, boy, play the blues' as an indication that the sax player Boots Randolph should begin soloing. It helps that Randolph plays the best he ever will in his life — he's otherwise best known for the minor hit Yakety Sax.

Thirty-five years after the event, RCA released an earlier version of Reconsider Baby, on The Complete 50s CD box set. It was recorded in December 1956 during the Million Dollar Quartet Sessions at Sun — Elvis was back in town, dropped by and sang a little with Sun's new stars, Carl Perkins, Jerry Lee Lewis and Johnny Cash.

Cash isn't there — he's gone shopping by this point. Carl Perkins starts off playing Jingle Bells for some reason and never gets better than basic, never approaches Scotty Moore's bluesy feel — which anyway is at its bluesiest on the later version. Jerry Lee Lewis, in his own inimitably egotistical way, just hits the piano keys harder and harder and harder, in a kind of pagan minimalism — quite without the charm of the tinkly sound Floyd Cramer's piano has on the 1960 version.

It's very early, very rough, scarcely developed enough to be called a jam. Yet one thing really stands out. You can clearly hear it's Elvis and his rhythm guitar playing that is pulling the song together, feeling its way towards giving it a shape of its own — in fact, pretty much the shape it took four years later on a Nashville dawn. A rare demonstration of Elvis the arranger and producer. 'Elvis produced his own records,' Bones Howe, the engineer on Hound Dog, has said. 'He came to the session, picked the songs, and if something in the arrangement was changed, he was the one to change it. Everything worked out spontaneously. Nothing was really rehearsed. Many of the important decisions normally made previous to a recording session were made during the session.'

Elvis cut Reconsider Baby one more time, a live version recorded at his first-ever concert in New York, the afternoon show of 10 June 1972. The arrangement has almost reverted to the Fulson original: it's led by the electric guitar and shaded by a horn section. When it comes time for the solo, Elvis shouts to his 1970s band-leader and guitarist, James Burton, just like he shouted to Boots Randolph a dozen years earlier. 'Play the blues, James. Play the blues,' he tells him. And what does James do? He does what he always does, plays a beautiful and measured but Country solo. Like other R&B tunes recorded by Elvis, it's often been derided as 'inauthentic' and 'derivative' — basically, the suggestion that a white southern boy couldn't sing the blues. Not that Elvis ever denied the background and history of what he was singing. In 1957, he had this to say to a reporter in Charlotte, North Carolina. 'Them critics don't like to see nobody doing any kind of music they don't know nuthin' about. The coloured folk been singing it and playing it just the way I'm doing now man, for more years than I know. Nobody paid it no mind till I goosed it up.'

But what about those black performers whose music he supposedly stole? Did they see Elvis as a thief in the night?

Little Richard, performer of Tutti Frutti, which Elvis covered in 1959: 'He was an integrator. Elvis was a blessing. They wouldn't let black music through. He opened the door for black music.'

Chuck Berry, three of whose songs Elvis covered and one of the most bitter and curmudgeonly men ever to have disgraced the planet: 'Blacks didn't have the airwaves Elvis had. He delivered what he obtained beautifully.'

Roy Brown, writer and performer of the original version of Elvis' second single, Good Rockin' Tonight: 'Elvis used to follow my band, from Tupelo to Vicksburg to Hattiesburg, and he just watched us. Later on, when I first saw him on The Ed Sullivan Show, all that wiggling and stuff, man, the blacks had been doing that for years. But there was something about Elvis that was different from the [white teen Pop] Fabians. Elvis could *sing*. And he had a heart. The guy was a beautiful human being. He had style and he had soul.'

And, lastly, Howlin' Wolf, three hundred pounds of former Delta sharecropper egomania. Elvis never recorded one of his songs but when asked to list his favourite blues singers, Mr Wolf replied: 'That other boy. What's his name? Somewhere out in California, that Hound Dog number. He *started* from the blues. If he stopped, he stopped. It's nothing to laugh at. He made his *pull* from the blues.' *ep*

I Feel So Bad
Written by: **Chuck Willis**
Recorded: **12 March 1961, Nashville**
First released: **c/w Wild In The Country, May 1961**

Around this time, immediately post-Army, Elvis really had a thing about 1954. Such A Night, Reconsider Baby and I Feel So Bad were all R&B hits that year which as well as marking Elvis' entry into showbiz, would also have been the last 'normal' year of his life.

By the time Elvis recorded I Feel So Bad, its writer had already been dead three years. Chuck Willis was a black Atlantan known as the Sheik Of The Blues and King Of The Stroll. He had a series of hits in the mid-1950s — an update of the old Blues, CC Rider song, What Am I Living For, I Feel So Bad and, immediately before his death, (I Don't Want To) Hang Up My Rock'n'Roll Shoes.

Elvis takes I Feel So Bad gently by the hand, smoothes it out a little, gives it more drive and pushes home the slightly self-pitying melancholy of its title — and the following line, 'just like a ballgame on a rainy day'. It must be said, though, that Boots Randolph, so authoritative on Reconsider Baby, turns in a hokey honk of a solo. *ep*

(K is for Kalamazoo)

The first place Elvis was spotted after he died — according to the Weekly World News, an American tabloid, which reported the sighting by 50-year-old 'mother of five' Louise Welling, non-Elvis fan and wife of a car assembly worker. She saw him twice, first in a grocery store, then — with her daughter and grandson — outside a Burger King restaurant. Having eaten, Elvis 'put on a pair of dark glasses, got into a small, light blue car and took off real fast.' Mrs Welling then added: 'Other people have seen him, but they are afraid to say anything.'

Can't Help Falling In Love
Written by: **George Weiss, Hugo Peretti, Luigi Creatore**
Recorded: **23 March 1961, Radio Recorders, Hollywood**
First released: **c/w Rock-A-Hula Baby, December 1961**

Can't Help Falling In Love is one of the few straightforward love songs Elvis recorded and by far the nicest. It is from Blue Hawaii, which my Elvis-fan eldest cousin, stuck with baby-sitting me, decided we should both go to the cinema to see — twice in the same afternoon. I remember lots of sand on the screen and being very bored — it was all about love and how can that compare to war and slapstick in a young boy's tastes? But I don't remember Can't Help Falling In Love, which is strange because it's the kind of simple, slightly leaden tune even a young boy could like.

It was written by a pair of New York Italian music business veterans who usually went by the joint byline, Hugo and Luigi. If that sounds like the front name of a money-laundering operation for the Mafia, it's because it was. In 1956, they co-founded Roulette Records with Maurice 'Mo'

Levy. The label — which had hits straightaway with Jackie and the Starlights, Buddy Knox and Frankie Lymon — was, in the words of the FBI, 'a source of ready cash for the Genovese Family and its leaders'. The Genoveses are known for their investments in gambling, loan-sharking, drugs, prostitution, the New York concrete business and Fulton Fish Market in lower Manhattan. In 1988, Levy was convicted on two counts of conspiracy to commit extortion, was sentenced to ten years — and immediately started appealing. He died two years later, not having served a day in jail.

Hugo and Luigi were cousins, middle-aged men. Hugo had worked as a trumpet player in Broadway shows. Luigi was a writer and novelist. But success came to them behind the scenes — as

A&R men, writers and producers, they sold maybe thirty million records. Their speciality was making Pop from slightly fringe material. Country singer Jimmie Rodgers was given Kisses Sweeter Than Wine. R&B stars the Isley Brothers crossed over with Shout. And the doo-wopping Tokens had a hit with the South African folk song, Wimoweh, which Hugo & Luigi retitled The Lion Sleeps Tonight.

Mostly, their speciality was exactly what Elvis has so often been accused of doing — white-breading rough and vibrant R&B songs. In 1955, they did this to LaVern Baker's Tweedle Dee — which Elvis played in his early live shows. So angry was Baker at Hugo and Luigi's version, which featured the (white) Georgia Gibbs, that she took her case to Congress to try and get the cover declared illegal. Undaunted, Hugo and Luigi took Etta James' R&B sex hit Wallflower and used Georgia Gibbs to bowdlerise it into a worldwide hit called Dance With Me (Henry).

In 1959, with Elvis away in the army, RCA records became worried about their lack of success in the pop charts so they hired Hugo and Luigi, paying them a million dollars. 'Unheard-of then,' said Luigi. They repaid the investment with a run of hits for Sam Cooke, taking the former R&B singer to the Pop mainland — whited him down, some say.

And when they were asked to provide a song for Elvis, they did what they always did — they borrowed someone else's inspiration. Like a lot of simple, instantly accessible tunes, Can't Help Falling In Love's was stolen — or rather 'adapted' from Plaisir D'Amour, an eighteenth century melody by Italian composer Giovanni Martini. Basically it's a bit of a plodder of a song. (Which is the reason it is one of the few Elvis ballads to become a nightclub standard. As with I Am What I Am and I Will Survive, everyone thinks they can sing it.) The lyrics — by George Weiss, a Tin Pan Alley hack, who also wrote Louis Armstrong's Wonderful World — also commence with a borrowed conceit. 'Wise men say, only fools rush in' is a blatant lift from Johnny Mercer's 1939 Only Fools Rush In.

In live shows, Elvis tended to perform it with all the swing of a sack of feathers. It became the song of benediction with which he closed his shows, taking scarves handed to him by an assistant and bestowing them on the eager hands reaching out from the front row. Yet the original has a pleading, winsome delicacy — Elvis' light voice trips beautifully across the clumpy rhythm.

Light and clean and somehow mysterious, it embodies the dream of Elvis the fragile, eternal supplicant at the altar of love. To start 'Shall I stay?' is to court rejection with almost baroque masochism. Bono, of all people, highlighted this on his version of the song, recorded for the film Honeymoon In Vegas but not used. In the background is the lightest of instrumentation and a recording of an Elvis press conference. In the foreground is little more than Bono's voice. At times, he sings in an almost castrato-like falsetto, echoing the resigned fatalism of the song's plea — who could be more inured to failure in love than a castrato? Elvis, I suppose. *ep*

(L is for Leg Wiggle)

The Leg Wiggle Controversy was a phrase first used by Ron Rosenbaum in a cover story for the New York Sunday Times magazine on 24 September 1995. It was about Elvisiana and Elvisianics — in other words, is Elvis a new religion? The Leg Wiggle Controversy focuses on the significance of Elvis' hip and thigh gyrations — sexual or spiritual?

In the academic corner stands Vernon Chadwick, Director of the now annual International Conference on Elvis Presley organised by the University of Mississippi's Centre For The Study Of Southern Culture (1966's event was subtitled Then Sings My Soul: Elvis And The Sacred South). Chadwick is an English professor with a modern English professor's way with words — he famously described Elvis as an 'assembler of clothing signifiers'. And as a good Mississippian he disdains what he sees as a Yankee distortion of the history and meaning of Elvis' hip movements. He wrote: 'With astonishing cultural illiteracy, New York critics of the 1950s mistook Elvis Presley's leg-shaking Rock 'n'Roll as an obscene striptease, when in fact his moves stemmed from the provincial subworlds of Southern Gospel, Country and Blues that combined spiritual exaltation with bodily release.' That is: it was the Lord's will moving Elvis' pelvis.

In the other corner of the Leg Wiggle Controversy was the Rev Howard Finster, an 'apocalyptic Folk artist' and self-proclaimed 'man of visions'. He too thought Elvis' pelvis was a gift from God but he believes it to have been an explicitly erotic gift. He says: 'Elvis was sent by God to revive sex, to stimulate sex and nature.' The Rev Finster learned this during a visit from Elvis the angel.

Elvis Alphabet

(Marie's The Name Of) His Latest Flame
Written by: **Doc Pomus, Mort Shuman**
Recorded: **26 June 1961**
First released: **c/w Little Sister, August 1961**

There's an echo here, right back to Elvis' first, amateur recording. As well as having the most splendid set of brackets in its title, (Marie's The Name Of) His Latest Flame tells a very similar story to That's When Your Heartaches Begin — i.e. what happens when your best friend and your best girl squeeze you out. In fact, the subject of best friends and best girls and the problems that can result when they mix is something of a running theme in ElvisWorld. A year before, he'd cut Girl Of My Best Friend. And his biggest record of the late 1960s was Suspicious Minds, which talks of 'an old friend passing by' — though, given what the future held, should probably have been 'a karate teacher passing by'.

It's sung in an unusually high, light voice and, like most of the other Pomus/Shuman songs that Elvis recorded, His Latest Flame gives real depth to teenage emotions — the intensity of which adults forget so easily as they get older. If high-school Pop could ever be genuinely cool, this is it. *ep*

Little Sister

Written by: **Doc Pomus, Mort Shuman**
Recorded: **26 June 1961**
First released: **c/w (Marie's The Name Of) His Latest Flame, August 1961**

Yet more bright, shiny high-school Pop, another instalment in the remarkable run of Pomus/Shuman master classes on how to fill a hit record with cleverness, while not letting your tongue get anywhere near your cheek. This one is straight out of the problem page of a teenage girls' magazine: Her Big Sis Is A Snog-Mad Boy Bandit! Or, as the song itself puts it, 'Little sister, don't you do what your big sister done'.

It's a studio confection that uses the session players' familiarity with each other's playing to create a (fake?) air of spontaneity. Like a lot of the Pomus/Shuman songs, it has the same Cuban-influenced drum rhythm as Phil Spector records — not unexpectedly, given that they both worked regularly with Spector. Driven along by the most fabulous sounding guitar, it both harks back to rockabilly — this is how the Johnny Burnette Rock'n'Roll Trio would have sounded if they'd been real Pop stars — and forward to Heavy Metal — this is what Led Zeppelin could have sounded like if they'd not thought length was so important. *ep*

(M is for Minnie May Presley)

Elvis' paternal grandmother who was born on 17 June, 1890. She outlived both her son Vernon and her grandson — whose birth she attended — only dying on 8 May, 1980. Hers is the one of the four gold and black gravestones in the Meditation Garden in the grounds of Graceland. (Actually, it's four and a quarter gravestones if you count the mini one for Elvis' stillborn twin, Jesse Garon.)

Suspicion
Written by: **Doc Pomus, Mort Shuman**
Recorded: **19 March 1962, RCA Studio B, Nashville**
First released: **on Pot Luck LP, June 1962**

Blowsy, slightly overwrought, tortured by imagined infidelity — Suspicion was a perfect Elvis song. Written by Pomus/Shuman, it was one of the last tracks recorded in a two-day Nashville session which also produced the last Leiber/Stoller Elvis hit, Just Tell Her Jim Said Hello — which, as a city-slicker parody of Country music, runs Cole Porter's Don't Fence Me In very close.

Like other songs he was cutting in the early 1960s — His Latest Flame and Return To Sender, for example — Suspicion is a Pop record with an R&B feel and an unusually original arrangement: Latinate rhythm plus harpsichord. The fact that Elvis was so very, very jealous in his own life obviously adds to both the power of his performance and the listener's voyeuristic amusement.

Dumped on an album called — with horrible accuracy — Pot Luck, it appeared again as the b-side of Kiss Me Quick. But it was Terry Stafford who had the hit with it, in 1964.

Many years later, Mort Shuman wrote about his time writing for Elvis. 'Doc and I never got to meet Elvis, but I didn't feel bad about it at the time. Now I realise that I would have at least liked to have his hand and told him who I was. As it is, he gave strangers Cadillacs — and I never even got a Christmas card.' *ep*

Return To Sender
Written by: **Otis Blackwell, Winfield Scott**
Recorded: **March 1962, Radio Recorders**
First released: **c/w Where Do You Come From, October 1962**

This is the first Elvis song I remember hearing. My aunt was a big fan — over the years she even came to look like Gladys. I'm sure that what I really liked about it — apart from the bouncy tune and story-telling quality that would engage any child — was simply that I was intrigued by the idea that you could post a letter and it could be returned to you. Like all children, I'd never really entertained the notion of impermanence. God knows how long it took me to figure out that the line about sending the letter back 'special D' was simply a truncation forced by line length — as bad a case of incompetent lyric-writing as I've ever seen. I always figured it had to be something far more magical, some kind of special service offered only by the American postal service.

Later, I discovered that Otis Blackwell was a man of many great notions for songs but never that great on the finishing touches. I also discovered that it was Elvis' only US million-seller between 1962 and 1969; that it was featured in Girls! Girls! Girls!; the tile song of which was originally written by Leiber and Stoller for the Coasters — who performed it with a lusty ease which quite escaped Elvis for once. And that, even more typically, the movie soundtrack included something called The Shrimp Song. *ep*

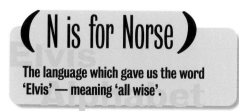

(N is for Norse)

The language which gave us the word 'Elvis' — meaning 'all wise'.

Viva Las Vegas

Written by: **Doc Pomus, Mort Shuman**
Recorded: **July 1963, Radio Reorders, Hollywood**
First released: **c/w What'd I Say, April 1964**

A great aria of wantingness, Pomus/Shuman's Viva Las Vegas is a gambler's scream of eternal hope: keep the dice tumbling, Lord, and I know, just know, I'll win in the end.

Viva Las Vegas was the second of Elvis' four significant encounters with the city itself. In 1956, he played a season there and bombed — why should anyone have thought middle-aged gamblers would be interested in Elvis Presley? In 1963, he recorded this song, in Hollywood, for the soundtrack of the movie of the same name; a duet version of it with his co-star Ann-Margaret has never been released. On 1 May, 1967, at 9.41am , in Las Vegas' Aladdin Hotel, he and Priscilla Ann Beaulieu were married by a Supreme Court Justice of the State of Nevada.

On 26 July 1969, at 10pm, in the Las Vegas' International Hotel, he returned to live performance for the first time since 1961, starting a seven-week engagement of two shows a night, seven nights a week which drew 100,000 people and grossed $1.5 million.

During that series of shows and subsequent Vegas runs, Elvis was often to be found at the tables — though not as often as Colonel Parker who was a very heavy loser. Yet that doesn't seem to explain the sheer ravenous joy about the place that he brings to the recording.

An explanation of that passion, though, is suggested by a passage from Freud's Dostoevsky And Parricide, a 1928 essay which examined the Russian novelist's addiction to gambling. Finding his clue in a short story by Stefan Zweig about an older woman's love for an obsessive gambler, Freud claims the story is based in the author's wish-fulfilment fantasy. 'The fantasy embodies a boy's wish that his mother should initiate him into sexual life in order to save him from the dreaded injuries caused by masturbation . . . The "vice" of masturbation is replaced by the addiction to gambling.' Elvis slept with his mother until he was 13.

The film of Viva Las Vegas, made as the US was succumbing to The Beatles, is blessed by Ann-Margaret, one of the few real women in Elvis' screen career. Her adult sexual energy brings to life what is otherwise a run-of-the-mill Elviser, redeemed only by some great car-racing footage and the knowledge that, off-screen as well as on, Elvis had an affair with Ann-Margaret — a serious, grown-up one, unusually for him. Here at last, thought his fans, was a Queen fit for a King. The picture of the pair of them getting married — her all in white, him in a dark suit with a white boutonnière — was only a film still, but she certainly thought she was going to marry him, saying so in a public announcement, rapidly denied by Colonel Parker. Elvis crept back to his child lover, Priscilla.

The Elvis movie business as a whole? By and large, Wittgenstein made the correct judgement in his Tractatus Logico-Philosophicus: 'Whereof one cannot speak , thereof one must be silent.' There are a couple of points though. Firstly, twins and twinning. In 1964's Kissin' Cousins, Elvis — who was of course originally part of a twinset — plays both Josh Morgan and Jodie Tatum. And a still from 1960's Flaming Star provided the basis for Andy Warhol's Elvis-as-twin-gunfighters painting, Double Elvis.

That's the evidence. Here is the thesis, as offered by clinical psychologist Peter Whitmer in a paper delivered at Harvard which considered Elvis as a 'Twinless twin'. Whitmer thinks the defining moment of Elvis' life was the stillbirth of his twin. That was the source of Elvis' pain and sense of loss, which he conveyed in his songs. Whitmer goes further, suggesting Elvis suffered from 'survivor guilt'. And, according to a piece by Ron Rosenbaum in the New York Sunday Times, 'every song he sang was really a duet with the ghost of his dead twin'.

Secondly, the Elvis film career which might have been. He tested for the young lead in The Rainmaker, which co-starred Katherine Hepburn and Burt Lancaster — Colonel Parker stopped him doing it and the part went to Earl Holliman. Robert Mitchum asked Elvis to be his co-star in Thunder Road — the part went to Mitchum's son, James. He was offered the Jon Voigt part in Midnight Cowboy. He was Barbra Streisand's first choice for her version of A Star Is Born — Kris Kristofferson did it instead.

Finally, Elvis' songwriters Jerry Leiber and Mike Stoller pushed the idea of their creating a musical version of Nelson Algren's lowlife novel A Walk On The Wild Side, to be scripted by Budd Schulberg (of On The Waterfront) and directed by Elia Kazan (also of On The Waterfront). Elvis' people told Leiber and Stoller where to get off. *ep*

Tomorrow Is A Long Time

Written by: **Bob Dylan**
Recorded: **26 May 1966, Nashville**
First released: **on Spinout LP, October 1966**

So deep were the dumps that Elvis' career was in at the time that Tomorrow Is A Long Time was scarcely noticed when it first came out. By late 1966, the average Elvis album was a jumble sale of tracks — songs from movies mixed with the results of occasional new studio sessions and old recordings from the 1950s. RCA just dumped it on the soundtrack album for Spinout, the last of 1966's three Elvis movies and one of the several in which he plays a racing driver.

It's an obscure Bob Dylan song written for his girlfriend Susie Rotolo — the woman with him on the cover of his Freewheelin' album — that was not issued by the writer himself till 1971. Elvis probably acquired it from the demo tapes of unreleased songs that Dylan's publishers hawked around looking for cover versions and which provided so many 1960s pop groups with hit records — Manfred Mann's Mighty Quinn, for example, and Julie Driscoll's This Wheel's On Fire.

It was cut at what was probably Elvis' most successful session of the mid-1960s. As well as this track, it also produced three notable cover versions — of the Clovers' Down In The Alley, the Drifters' Fools Fall In Love and Ketty Lester's Love Letters. (He also covered Bing Crosby's cod-Hawaiian Beyond The Reef, but we shall let that pass.)

It's true, at first thought anyway, that Dylan and Elvis make a strange mixture — the King of Rock'n'Roll with his Cadillacs and gold suit teamed with the Prince of Protest in his poor-boy denims; the raging, overweight southern Pentecostalist versus the neurotic Jewish kid from the north country.

But the links between the two are more striking and more interesting. Both grew up on the same kind of Blues and traditional music — which other two big-time pop stars could you find who've both cut Froggie Goes A' Courtin? Dylan started his pop career hankering after being Elvis. Hearing Elvis for the first time, he once said, was 'like busting out of jail,' and one of his first studio recordings was That's All Right, (Mama) Plus, both Elvis and Bob liked drugs and riding their Triumph 500 motorbikes — though only Elvis had a fatal accident with the former and only Bob had a near-fatal accident on the latter.

Fittingly, Tomorrow Is A Long Time sounds like no other Elvis recording. The vocal is low, quiet, the backing is reserved. James Burton's flowing guitar has the high, ringing tone of a Dobro — though, strangely, he does keep trying to play R&B licks. What it sounds like more than anything else is Elvis pretending to be Dylan. Or rather, Elvis trying the mantle of Folk-singer on for size. It fits, there's no doubt about that, but Elvis seems quite content to leave it at that. He doesn't want to be Dylan, he just wants to see how it feels to be Bob.

Over the years, he sang other Dylan songs in concert — All I Really Want To Do, Blowin' In The Wind, It Ain't Me Babe, Mr Tambourine Man, She Belongs To Me. But he never really sounds like he's properly woken up for them. Only twice more, on two recordings made in early-1971, did he seem to concentrate. On a 'jam' version of Don't Think Twice, It's Alright — also written for Susie Rotolo — and on a very sketchy take of I Shall Be Released. 'Dylan', he announces, at the end of it, deliberately and authoritatively paying his respects.

Dylan had already returned the compliment, when Tomorrow Is A Long Time was first released. 'Elvis recorded a song of mine,' he said. 'That's the one recording I treasure most.' *ep*

(O is for 'OK, I won't')

Elvis' last words. His last girlfriend, Ginger Alden, former Miss Traffic Safety and Miss Mid-South, had told him not to fall asleep reading in the toilet. His last book was either The Scientific Search For The Face Of Jesus by Frank Adams or The Shroud Of Turin by Ian Wilson. His last meal, according to Goldman, was hamburgers and French fries at dawn the previous day, prepared by his cook Mary Jenkins — despite her urgings, Elvis wouldn't touch his food on the day of his death. Other sources say a different cook, Pauline Nicholson, served him ice cream and cookies at 4am — just the day after he'd had a cavity filled, by the way.

US Male

Written by: **Jerry Reed**
Recorded: **17 January 1968, RCA Nashville**
First released: **c/w Stay Away, March 1968**

That US Male made it on to the bootleg album, Elvis' Greatest Shit! (for further details of this must-not buy, see Elvis alphabet, Y is for Yoga Is As Yoga Does), must be down to two things: the achingly bad pun of the title and an atrocious moment in the spoken intro which forcibly rhymes 'born' and 'Mississippi morn'. Because those calluses aside, it's clearly the starting point of Elvis' 1968 rebirth.

Country guitarist and songwriter Jerry Reed had been invited to work with Elvis the previous September on a Nashville session. Starting with Reed's own Guitar Man, Elvis was reintroduced to the delights of R&B for the first time in years, cutting both Jimmy Reed's Blues shuffle, Big Boss Man, and Tommy Tucker's celebration of a ghetto Saturday night, High Heel Sneakers. Guitar Man was issued as a single and became a minor hit in Britain — where the Elvis appreciation factor was still high — but inevitably flopped in the US.

US Male, however, brought Elvis back to the charts. A bouncy Country Rock song — at a time when Country Rock was a phrase still a couple of years from being born — US Male is pretty much a glossed-up version of Jerry Reed's own life. A couple of years Elvis' junior, Reed was an Atlantan who got into the music business in 1955, writing Crazy Legs for Gene Vincent. A lightning-fast guitar picker, he became a first-choice session musician in Nashville, then moved on to making his own records. Guitar Man was a hit for him in 1967. Both Amos Moses and When You're Hot, You're Hot followed in 1972, after which he also took up a side career as a professional good ol' boy in Burt Reynolds movies — WW And The Dixie Dance Kings, for example, and Smokey The Bandit. He also penned one of Country music's greatest parenthetical statements, 1982's She's Got The Goldmine (I Got The Shaft). *ep*

Trouble/Guitar Man
Trouble written by: **Jerry Leiber, Mike Stoller**
Guitar Man written by: **Jerry Reed**
Recorded: **June 1968, Burbank**
First released: **on NBC TV Special, December 1968**

This is how the TV comeback started, with Elvis announcing: 'if you're looking for trouble, you've come to the right place'. His belief in the importance of the moment and in what he was singing overwhelmed the hokiness of the lyric to this stomping Blues. Jerry Leiber, the man who wrote the words to Trouble, described it as a send-up, saying Elvis Presley was the only person who could have taken it seriously. He added 'There's something laughable there. I mean, if you get Memphis Slim or John Lee Hooker singing it, it sounds right, but Elvis did not sound right to us.' Us being Leiber and his co-writer Mike Stoller.

They wrote the song back in early-1958, for Elvis' fourth movie King Creole. His co-star was Dolores Hart (nee Hicks), who also played opposite him in his second movie, Loving You. They dated, he called her Whistle Britches, she wrote an article headlined 'What It's Like To Kiss Elvis' and — reportedly — confessed to Elvis' friends that she was still in love with the King. Retiring from the movie business in 1963, she is now Mother Superior at the Convent Of Regina Laudis in Bethlehem, Connecticut.

Guitar Man, the second song of the pair which kicked off the TV show, was one Elvis had recorded the previous autumn — though only after his people had lost their usual argument with the songwriter over the credit. Jerry Reed — who had already had a hit with the song himself — wouldn't budge, insisted on keeping his rights and finally prevailed. When Elvis came to record it, he wanted exactly the same guitar sound that Reed had on his version. But they couldn't get it. So producer Felton Jarvis called Reed, who was away on a fishing trip, into the studio. He arrived looking like a 'sure-enough Alabama wildman'. But he gave Elvis the guitar sound he was after. *ep*

Blue Christmas/One Night

Blue Christmas written by: **Bill Hayes and Jay Johnson**
One Night written by: **Dave Bartholomew, Pearl King**
Recorded: **June 1968, Burbank**
First released: **on Elvis TV Special, November 1968**

This must be where MTV got the whole idea for Unplugged. Producer Steve Binder came up with the idea of a semi-acoustic session featuring Elvis and his original band — guitarist Scotty Moore and drummer DJ Fontana, that is; bassist Bill Black had died in 1965 — playing on a boxing ring sized stage surrounded by an audience on all four sides. As so often in TV, not all was quite what it seemed. The other two 'musicians' on the stage were nothing of the kind. They were Charlie Hodge (nicknames Slewfoot and Waterhead), a pal of Elvis' since the army, and Alan Fortas (nickname Hog Ears), a member of the Memphis Mafia who'd been a bodyguard for Elvis since King Creole days.

Elvis was 33 years old — the age, of course, at which Jesus died — and dressed in black leather, a fetishist's wet dream. Some of what he chose to sing reached back to the Sun days — his own That's All Right, Trying To Get To You and a rattling treatment of Rufus Thomas' Tiger Man. But even the newer songs sounded like they were being overseen by Sam Phillips. Blue Christmas was a hit for (white) country star Ernest Tubb in 1949 and for (black) R&B star Billy Eckstine in 1950. Elvis first recorded it in Septmber 1957 at Radio Recorders in Hollywood at the session supervised by Leiber and Stoller which produced the whole of the Elvis' Christmas Album. Strangely, given how it's become an annual seasonal classic, it didn't come out as a single till 1964. Even more strangely, on this live version, as Elvis riffs away on his guitar, one of his sidekicks shouts out 'Play it dirty!'

Which sentiment would have been more suited to the second song of the linked pair, One Night, a song of bitter sexual regret written and first recorded by Smiley Lewis in November 1955. That wasn't his real name, of course. He chose Smiley Lewis because he loathed his given name, Amos Overton Lemmon. (You can see his point.) New Orleans had many great R&B pianists in the immediate post-war period — Fats Domino, Archibald, Huey Smith, Professor Longhair. Smiley Lewis, though, was a guitarist. He made a string of loud, rough, memorable Crescent City R&B records — Real Gone Lover, Shame, Shame, Shame, the original Blue Monday — but his only hit was with I Hear You Knocking, as dosed with rockin' pneumonia and the boogie woogie flu by Huey Smith's piano.

One Night is a lover's memoir, often referred to as One Night (Of Sin) because it sets up the next line so well: 'is what I'm now paying for'. (Quite what resulted from the night of sin is never clear. Unwanted pregnancy, social disease, wife finding out — it could be any or all of them.)

Understandably, the subject matter presented problems for Elvis on his first, 1957 version of it, cut at Radio Recorders in Hollywood. The solution was linguistic. 'Sin' turned to 'love' and 'paying' to 'praying'. Thus: one night of love is what I'm now praying for.

Cleverly, he retained the sexual charge of Smiley Lewis' original by singing the new lyrics with the meaning of the old. Amusingly, it first appeared as the flip of I Got Stung. Then, in 1983, RCA finally released Elvis' first attempt at the song, cut a month earlier. This version featured the original words but didn't carry a fraction of the bowdlerised version's sense of sin. Which is the best advert for censorship I've ever heard. **ep**

Baby What You Want Me To Do
Written by: **Jimmy Reed**
Recorded: **June 1968, Burbank**
First released: **on Elvis TV Special, November 1968**

There were two significant Reeds in Elvis' late-1960s comeback. White Jerry Reed wrote US Male and Guitar Man. Black Jimmy Reed provided Big Boss Man — which Elvis recorded in late 1967 — and Baby What You Want Me To Do. Ten years Elvis' senior, Jimmy Reed was a fellow Mississippian whose shuffling blues caught the taste of black and white Americans around the start of the 1960s — Baby What You Want Me To Do was a hit in 1959, Big Boss Man in 1960 and Bright Lights, Big City in 1961. Ironically, by 1968, Jimmy Reed was probably best known through cover versions of his material by English invasion groups — the Rolling Stones in particular.

Unlike the other old R&B songs played in the TV show's black-leather-suited 'jam' session, Baby What You Want Me To Do is clarified by a proper arrangement, Elvis himself on lead guitar, a horn section and Scotty Moore's last contribution to Elvis' music. Having played guitar on every record Elvis had made, Scotty Moore was dumped. The man whose 1964 solo LP was aptly titled The Guitar That Changed The World never saw Elvis again. **ep**

(P is for publishing)

I checked how many Elvis books are available from amazon.com, 'The world's biggest bookstore'. Four hundred and twenty four at the last count. There are reference books, of course — invaluably helpful I've found them too. The well–known biographies — likewise. Memoirs — by former lovers, bodyguards, his nurse and a fellow soldier. Personal narratives — Elvis Is Dead And I Don't Feel Too Good Myself. Recipe books — for peanut butter fans only. Fiction — Zip Six: A Novel. Conspiracy theories — Top Secret: The Untold Story Of Elvis Presley's Secret FBI Files, for example. Academic texts — The Inner Elvis: A Psychological Biography Of

Elvis Aaron Presley Vol 1 and Elvis (American Structural Readers: Stage1).
Others are even more specialised, to say the least — The Day Elvis Met Nixon, say, or Elvis Presley Calls His Mother After The Ed Sullivan Show or Did Elvis Sing In Your Hometown?. Some must be a joke but, on the other hand, just might not be — The Gospel Of Elvis: Containing The Testament And Apocrypha Including All The Greater Themes Of The King has to come in that category, as does Elvis For President: Committee To Elect The King and, I guess, Alien Pregnant By Elvis. Others are just plain baffling — Elvis In Aspic, for instance.

If I Can Dream
Written by: **W Earl Brown**
Recorded: **29 June 1968, Western Recorders**
First released: **c/w Edge Of Reality, November 1968**

The link with that other great dream of the 1960s — Martin Luther King's — is inescapable. When Elvis recorded If I Can Dream, as the finale of his TV comeback special, Dr King had been dead less than three months — assassinated on 4 April on a balcony of the Hotel Lorraine in Elvis' home town of Memphis. Dr King was there to give his backing to the (mostly black) sanitation workers in their strike against the city authorities. The precariousness of racial tension in Memphis can be seen in a photograph taken the day after Dr King's death. In a crush of (white) priests, reporters and city officials, Mayor Henry Loeb reaches across his desk to shake hands with a preacher, the (black) Rev P Toney. The report says: 'The ministers were impressed with Loeb's cordiality in the face of such a potentially uncomfortable confrontation. But Loeb gave no indication he was willing to compromise with the strikers.' What the ministers couldn't have known is something the photograph shows. Tucked away beneath Loeb's desk is a shotgun.

Then, on 5 June, Robert Kennedy was assassinated while campaigning for President, in the basement of a hotel in Los Angeles — not that far from the city of Burbank where Elvis taped his TV special.

The eventual choice of If I Can Dream came at the end of a very long period of argument. All along, Colonel Parker had wanted the show to be a Christmas special. His idea was that Elvis should stick to hymns and carols for the show. So he was, understandably, worried about the idea being pushed by the producer, Steve Binder: that the finale should be Elvis walking up to the camera and saying: 'I care!'

A noxious, empty, luvvie notion, of course. But, given the hokum the Colonel got Elvis to do over the years, it's unlikely his objection to Binder's idea was aesthetic. It would have been rather more hard-headed than that — and correctly so. He was the manager, that was how he was meant to think, that was what his percentage was for. Elvis' career was in trouble: his last top ten hit had been five years ago: his last number one, seven years ago: the movie money river had dried up. So what was the point ... or rather, where was the profit in alienating a good part of Elvis' core audience by choosing a 'socially aware' song?

So the Colonel shot back with his own piece of hokum, suggesting Elvis finish with I Believe, a ghastly piece of cod-gospel that he'd recorded in January 1957 for the Peace In The Valley EP — it was a big hit in America for Frankie Laine, a specialist in country weepies, and in Britain for the Bachelors, a harmony trio who came from Ulster and always wore sweaters.

Understandably, Binder rejected that and came up with another suggestion — a new 'socially aware' song of such lyrical vagueness that they could slip it by the Colonel. W Earl Brown was sent away with the brief to write it, overnight. The next morning, Brown sang it to Elvis, with the show's musical director William Goldenberg on piano. Elvis agreed to do it. The Colonel and representatives from NBC and RCA were in the next office. Binder called them in to hear the song. Unfortunately for the Colonel, the execs loved it.

Elvis recorded it alone onstage with a hand mike, dressed in a white, fashionably double-breasted suit. He looked, as he was meant to, like a hip preacher — he even did James Brown-style knee-drops. And then he re-recorded it, overdubbing the vocal in a darkened studio, writhing around the floor, screaming out the lyrics, investing their simplicities with meaning. Knowing what we do about the state of Elvis' personal and emotional problems, it makes just as much sense as a cry of private misery as it does as a call for social justice. Even Albert Goldman was impressed, comparing Elvis' performance to that of one of his great black heroes: 'so reminiscent of the blind Ray Charles crying out in anguish from his darkness'.

That the emotional drive of the performance is personal rather than social does make sense. There is no evidence at all that Elvis ever showed any interest whatsoever in the Civil Rights movement. In fact, despite the fact that he always credited his black influences and peers, his feelings were close to those of a lot of Southerners at that time. Blacks, Catholics and Jews, he felt the same about all of them — hating the group while liking the individual. He made racist remarks to his black band members — yet defended them against other racists. He thought Catholics were demons — yet married one. He believed

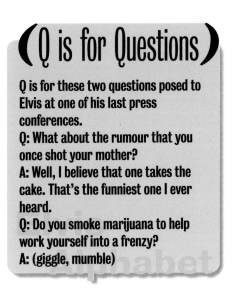

Q is for Questions

Q is for these two questions posed to Elvis at one of his last press conferences.
Q: What about the rumour that you once shot your mother?
A: Well, I believe that one takes the cake. That's the funniest one I ever heard.
Q: Do you smoke marijuana to help work yourself into a frenzy?
A: (giggle, mumble)

Jews were an international conspiracy — yet had many close Jewish friends, worked happily with Jews and gave widely to Jewish charities. Common sentiments but not those of a social crusader.

No, whatever others might have heard in If I Can Dream, Elvis found a sense of personal deliverance. Bones Howe had worked on Elvis sessions since 1957 and was engineer and co-producer of the TV special. He reports that when Elvis had watched the tape of the whole show several times, he said: 'You know, I'll never sing another song that I don't believe in. I'm never going to make another movie that I don't believe in.'

Not true, of course, but If I Can Dream did lead to a brief flurry of Elvis 'message' songs — both In The Ghetto and Don't Cry Daddy were recorded early the following year — and became Elvis' biggest hit single for some years. Which must have really pissed off Binder and Howe who had expected to be cut in on the royalty payments only to run up against the Colonel's business acumen.

The TV special was broadcast on NBC at 9pm on 3 December 1968 and achieved the highest ratings of the week. It was sponsored by the sewing machine manufacturer, Singer, who paid $400,000 for the first showing and $275,000 for a repeat. And it achieved its objective of relaunching Elvis' career. Within weeks, he was back in a Memphis studio for the first time since 1955. Within months, he was playing his first live shows, in Las Vegas, since his 1961 charity performance at Pearl Harbour. *ep*

Long Black Limousine
Written by: **Bobby George, Vern Stovall**
Recorded: **13 January 1969, American Sound Studios, 827 Thomas Street, Memphis**
First released: **on From Elvis In Memphis, June 1969**

Having started his comeback in a Nashville studio with Jerry Reed and solidified it in a Burbank studio with his old pals from the Sun days, Elvis now confirmed it in Memphis with an entirely new band, recording in his home town for the first time since Sun days. The band had been put together by Stan Kesler, who had written five songs for Elvis over the years, starting with the flip of his third single, I'm Left, You're Right, She's Gone. Known as the 827 Thomas Street Band — after American Studio's address — they'd played on Sam The Sham's Woolly Bully and eccentric soul singer James Carr's work for the Goldwax label, then moved on to work pretty much exclusively for American Studio owner and producer, Chips Moman.

(So Stan Kesler put a new session band together, the Dixie Flyers, which Atlantic's Jerry Wexler stole and relocated in Miami — where they first excelled themselves on Aretha Franklin's Grammy-winning Don't Play That Song, then made a career switch into drug-taking. A third Kesler band was stolen by Memphis studio owner Seymour Rosenberg. This time Stan gave up and went to work full-time for Chips. These days, Stan plays rockabilly around Memphis, as part of the Sun Rhythm Section.)

By the time Elvis arrived at American, the studio was on a three-year run of 122 hits, for a whole range of artists, from Neil Diamond to Dusty Springfield to the Box Tops to Wilson Pickett. Understandably, they were full of themselves. Horn player Wayne Jackson: 'I mean, we were thrilled about Elvis, but it wasn't like doing Neil Diamond.'

Elvis believed he was up to the challenge. As Felton Jarvis, his longtime A&R man at RCA Records, told Peter Guralnick, 'He just wanted to try something different. He'd been doing the same old thing for a long time. He just decided he would like to try a different approach. Try to prove himself.'

Long Black Limousine was the first track Elvis recorded at American. A Gospel/Country weepie, it was written by two Country singer-songwriters, Bobby George and former slaughterhouseman Vern Stovall, who had worked together since 1961 when Stovall made the first recording of it. It's the story of a young woman who dreams of returning to her home town in glory and the long black limousine of the title. She does, of course, only it's a hearse.

Elvis performs it with unusual dramatic reticence. The parallel with his own life is as poignant as it is obvious. Though the limos at his funeral, all sixteen of them, were in fact white. *ep*

❪R is for Rock'n'Roll❫

Of course. One day, someone complimented Sam Phillips on his
talents as a record producer. 'Producing?' said Sam. 'I don't know
anything about producing records. But if you want to make some
Rock'n'Roll music, I can reach down and pull it out of your asshole.'

In The Ghetto
Written by: **Mac Davis**
Recorded: **21 January 1969, American**
First released: **c/w Any Day Now, April 1969**

It was a time of 'message' songs, from the Beatles' Revolution to Marvin Gaye's What's Going On. Elvis wasn't stupid. He didn't — to coin a phrase of that well-known message songwriter, Bob Dylan – need a weatherman to know which way the wind blew. He'd seen how well If I Can Dream had been received, both on his NBC TV special and as a single.

On this first recording session in a Memphis studio for the first time since his Sun days, he wasn't going to blow the opportunity to solidify his 'comeback' by not seeming 'contemporary'. So, despite what various members of his entourage have since said, it's unlikely he had that many doubts about recording such an upfront piece of 'social commentary' as In The Ghetto.

Mac Davis was a young Texan from Lubbock, the same town as Buddy Holly, with first-hand knowledge of what he was writing about — his first job was in the Georgia probation service. After a failed attempt at being a Rock'n'Roll star himself at the turn of the 1960s, he'd stayed in the music business. First he was an executive — including a spell as regional manager for the

Beatles' first US label, the black-owned Vee-Jay Records. Then he turned to writing. He had hits with Lou Rawls and Glen Campbell in 1967. And, in 1968, Colonel Parker gave Elvis a couple of songs that Mac had written with Billy Strange. A Little Less Conversation made it into the movie Live A Little, Love A Little and the more obviously messagey Clean Up Your Own Backyard was used in the wonderfully bracketed The Trouble With Girls (And How To Get Into It).

Credit for bringing In The Ghetto to the Memphis sessions, though, is claimed by Chips Moman and Felton Jarvis, the latter the nearest thing Elvis had to an A&R man or producer for a good part of his career. It was the lead track of a seventeen-song tape that had been put together not for Elvis but for Bill Medley of the Righteous Brothers. (At one point, Chips wanted to cut it with a black ex-football star he had signed.)

Reggie Young played guitar on it. 'Elvis was just really into it,' he told Peter Guralnick. 'I remember it being stopped a few times — he just wanted to do it better. It was like he was finally doing a song with some meaning to it, with some soul — it would have to turn him on. By this time, he was really enthused about what he was doing, he really cared. Instead of it just being a party — you know, just go into the studio and have a party — he was really trying.'

Sung in the low part of Elvis' register, the conviction of the performance and the delicacy of the arrangement wash away any lingering cynicism about the earnestness of the lyrics or about Elvis' lack of experience in latter years of babies crying on cold and windy mornings in a Chicago ghetto. If pop stars' political gesturing — Live Aid, Free Nelson Mandela and so on — later became both a cliché and cynical career opportunity, In The Ghetto just about lets me suspend my disbelief.

The a-side of the first single released from the American sessions, it gave Elvis his first US Top Ten in four years. Its follow-up was splendidly cynical — the other Mac Davis song Elvis recorded, Clean Up Your Own Backyard. As Elvis movies were doing such indifferent business by this time, soundtrack albums weren't even released — so this was Clean Up Your Own Backyard's record debut. It peaked at 45.

The next-but-one Elvis single was yet another Mac Davis song, the cute Don't Cry Daddy. Recorded five days before In The Ghetto, it was inspired by Mac's son Scotty telling him not to get so upset by TV coverage of the Vietnam War and became Elvis' last hit of the 1960s, reaching number 6 in November 1969.

Naturally, Davis then launched a solo career which, just as naturally, took straight off — number one with Baby Don't Get Hooked On Me and a big hit with Rock'n'Roll (I Gave You The Best Years Of My Life) — then ebbed away. In 1979, he signed for Casablanca just in time to watch it go bankrupt. And in 1980 he wrote It's Hard To Be Humble, perhaps best known in the version recorded by Max Bygraves. *ep*

Suspicious Minds
Written by: **Mark James**
Recorded: **23 January 1969, American Studios**
First released: **c/w You'll Think Of Me, September 1969**

The last song recorded in the first set of sessions at American, Suspicious Minds was a strange prefiguring of the jealousy that would soon tear apart his marriage. It is also, unsurprisingly, a favourite of that other Southern mama's boy, Jack Stanton, who is a kind of properly educated Elvis, with his taste for life's fleshy pleasures (fresh and female as well as porky and cooked).

Written, and recorded the previous year, by Mark James (who also wrote Always On My Mind and Moody Blue for Elvis), Suspicious Minds is given a big, blaring soul setting — with Reggie Young playing a guitar given to him by Scotty Moore, who had just been dumped after fifteen years as Elvis' guitarist.

By the time Elvis came to record it, the song had already been the cause of yet another of the rows over publishing rights which disfigured so many Elvis sessions. This one nearly blew the whole two weeks' work. Suspicious Minds' copyright was with Press Music, the publishing company of the producer — and American Studio's owner — Chips Moman. On the sleeve notes of The Memphis Record, Peter Guralnick records that when Elvis' people, as usual, asked for a 25 per cent kickback, Moman asked them to leave. 'I'll tell you what,' he said. 'You can just consider this a very expensive demo session. As a matter of fact, I'll do it for free. But don't you ever come back in this studio again.' Elvis' people backed down and Elvis taped his real comeback hit, his first number one since 1962's Good Luck Charm — with a song whose ending, suitably, is a long fade followed by a sudden, unexpected comeback. *ep*

(S is for Scatter)

Elvis' pet chimpanzee who lived the life of a Country song in Graceland. When Elvis got bored with Scatter, the Memphis Mafia took over his care, dressing him in human clothes and introducing him to hard liquor. He became a violent alcoholic and died of cirrhosis of the liver.

ELVIS The Memphis Record EXTRA

DIGITALLY REMASTERED

1969: YEAR IN REVIEW

ACADEMY AWARD WINNERS

- Best Picture
  Midnight Cowboy
- Best Actor
  John Wayne, True Grit
- Best Actress
  Maggie Smith, The Prime Of Miss Jean Brodie
- Best Supporting Actor
  Gig Young, They Shoot Horses, Don't They?
- Best Supporting Actress
  Goldie Hawn, Cactus Flower

GRAMMY WINNERS

- Record Of The Year
  Aquarius/Let The Sunshine In, 5th Dimension
- Album Of The Year
  Blood, Sweat & Tears, Blood, Sweat & Tears
- Song Of The Year
  Games People Play, Joe South
- Best New Artist
  Crosby, Stills And Nash

COMEBACK Elvis Presley, as he appeared in December 1968 NBC television special

- ☐ **PRESLEY RETURNS HOME FOR FIRST MEMPHIS SESSIONS SINCE MID-1950's**
- ☐ **FIRST MAN WALKS ON MOON**
- ☐ **HALF MILLION IN ATTENDANCE AT WOODSTOCK FESTIVAL**
- ☐ **NEW YORK METS WIN WORLD SERIES**
- ☐ **NIXON SWORN IN AS NATION'S 37TH PRESIDENT**
- ☐ **JETS UPSET COLTS IN SUPER BOWL III**

THE YEAR'S NO. 1 HITS

I Heard It Through The Grapevine – Marvin Gaye
Crimson And Clover – Tommy James & The Shondells
Everyday People – Sly & The Family Stone
Dizzy – Tommy Roe
Aquarius/Let The Sunshine In – 5th Dimension
Get Back – Beatles
Love Theme From 'Romeo & Juliet' – Henry Mancini
In The Year 2525 – Zager & Evans
Honky Tonk Women – Rolling Stones
Sugar, Sugar – Archies
I Can't Get Next To You – Temptations
Suspicious Minds – Elvis Presley
Wedding Bell Blues – 5th Dimension
Come Together – Beatles
Na Na Hey Hey Kiss Him Goodbye – Steam
Leaving On A Jet Plane – Peter, Paul and Mary
Someday We'll Be Together – Diana Ross & The Supremes

-ELVIS PRESLEY-

COMMEMORATIVE

-ISSUE-

CONTENTS

1. **STRANGER IN MY OWN HOME TOWN** (P. Mayfield) 4:39
2. **POWER OF MY LOVE** (B. Giant-B. Baum-F. Kaye) 2:36
3. **ONLY THE STRONG SURVIVE** (K. Gamble-L. Huff-J. Butler) 2:42
4. **ANY DAY NOW** (B. Bacharach-B. Hilliard) 2:55
5. **SUSPICIOUS MINDS** (M. James) 3:24
6. **LONG BLACK LIMOUSINE** (V. Stovall-B. George) 3:38
7. **WEARIN' THAT LOVED ON LOOK** (D. Frazier-A.L. Owens) 2:42
8. **I'LL HOLD YOU IN MY HEART (TILL I CAN HOLD YOU IN MY ARMS)** (T. Dilbeck-V. Horton-E. Arnold) 4:32
9. **AFTER LOVING YOU** (E. Miller-J. Lantz) 2:58
10. **RUBBERNECKIN'** (D. Jones-B. Warren) 2:08
11. **I'M MOVIN' ON** (H. Snow) 2:53
12. **GENTLE ON MY MIND** (J. Hartford) 3:19
13. **TRUE LOVE TRAVELS ON A GRAVEL ROAD** (D. Frazier-A.L. Owens) 2:44
14. **IT KEEPS RIGHT ON A-HURTIN'** (J. Tillotson) 2:38
15. **YOU'LL THINK OF ME** (M. Shuman) 4:09
16. **MAMA LIKED THE ROSES** (J. Christopher) 2:32
17. **DON'T CRY DADDY** (M. Davis) 2:48
18. **IN THE GHETTO** (M. Davis) 2:46
19. **THE FAIR IS MOVING ON** (D. Fletcher-D. Flett) 3:06
20. **INHERIT THE WIND** (E. Rabbitt) 3:11
21. **KENTUCKY RAIN** (E. Rabbitt-D. Heard) 3:25
22. **WITHOUT LOVE (THERE IS NOTHING)** (D. Small) 2:55
23. **WHO AM I?** (B. Goodman) 3:20

MUSICIANS

RCA

BAND

Reggie Young, guitar; Bobby Wood, piano; Bobby Emmons, organ; Tommy Cogbill, Mike Leech, bass; Gene Chrisman, drums; Ed Kollis, harmonica; John Hughey, steel guitar. Additional piano by Ronnie Milsap (C-5) and Elvis Presley (B-1, B-4).

BACKING VOCALS

Mary Greene, Mary Holladay, Susan Pilkington, Donna Thatcher, Sandy Posey (C-5) and Ronnie Milsap (D-6) in Memphis.
Joe Babcock, Dolores Edgin, Millie Kirkham, Sonja Montgomery and Hurshel Wiginton in Nashville (C-2, C-3, D-2, D-6).

HORNS

Wayne Jackson, Dick Steff, R.F. Taylor, trumpets; Andrew Love, J.P. Luper, Glen Spreen, Jackie Thomas, saxophones; Jack Hale, Ed Logan, Gerald Richardson, Jackie Thomas, trombones; Tom Clauer, Joe D'Gerolamo, french horns, in Memphis. Norman Putnam, Bobby Shaw, Art Vasquez, trumpets; Kenneth Atkins, Johnny Boucie, Archie Le Cogar, trombones, in Las Vegas (A-5).

STRINGS

Arnold Blumberg, Albert Edelman, Nate Evans, Ed Freudberg, Noel Gilbert, Gloria Hendricks, Anne Oldham, Hal Saunders, Robert Snyder, Ann Sparbeck, violins; Mike Leech, Fred Lowing, Nino Rusarito, Mary Snyder, Glen Spreen, Vernon Taylor, John Weblan, violas; Pamela Blackwell, Anne Kendall, Joshua Langfur, Peter Sparbeck, cellos, in Memphis.
Brenton Banks, George Binkley, Solie Fott, Lilian Hunt, Pieter Menard, Akira Nagai, violins; Marvin Chantry, Gary Vanosdale, violas; Byron Bach, Sadao Harada, cellos, in Nashville (C-2, C-3, D-2, D-6)

CREDITS

Recorded at American Studios
Memphis, Tennessee
January and February, 1969
Original Sessions Produced by Chips Moman
Arranged by Glen Spreen and Mike Leech
Some Overdubs Produced by Felton Jarvis
Nashville Session Arranged by Don Tweedy
Engineer: Al Pachuki
Assisted by Roy Shockley
This Compilation
A&R Director: Gregg Geller
Marketing Director
Don Wardell
Audio Restoration by Rick Rowe
Mastered by Jack Adelman
Liner Notes by Peter Guralnick
Art Direction: Ria Lewerke
Design: Pietro Alfieri
Photos courtesy of Michael Ochs Archives

PD86221

For the house band at the tiny American Studios at 827 Thomas St., in a run-down section of Memphis, it wasn't any big deal. Monday, January 13, marked the beginning of yet another session for yet another artist evidently seeking the American magic. It was 1969, and the studio was in the midst of a string of 122 charts hits that would be cut over a period of three years with virtually the same rhythm section (Reggie Young on guitar; Bobby

Wood and Bobby Emmons on keyboards; Tommy Cogbill and Mike Leech on bass; Gene Chrisman on drums). Neil Diamond had just finished a session there in the course of which he had recorded 'Brother Love's Travelling Salvation Show', 'Sweet Caroline', and 'Holly Holy'. Even if the next artist had not been mired in a long-standing commercial slump, it was difficult at this point to tell just what he was capable of since he had been cut off from contact with the public and his fellow musicians for so long. Everyone in the studio knew who the singer was, they had all grown up on his music, and he was, of course, a native Memphian, but perhaps for these reasons, too, it

seemed as if this session could represent little more than a nostalgic bow to the past. "I mean, we were terrified about Elvis," said horn player Wayne Jackson, "but it wasn't like doing Neil Diamond."

For Chips Moman, American's founder, owner, chief engineer, songwriter, and occasional guitar player,

the upcoming session promised as many headaches as thrills. Like the house band, he knew of and admired Elvis ("I had met him, but that's all — I had been around Memphis for a long time"), but he was also aware that no one had really "produced" an Elvis session in years, and he himself (full story inside.)

TROUBLE Elvis Presley as he appeared in the 1968 feature 'The Trouble With Girls (And How To Get Into It)'

Stranger In My Own Home Town
Written by: **Percy Mayfield**
Recorded: **17 Febuary, 1969, American studio**
First released: **on From Memphis To Vegas LP, November 1969**

More than anything else Elvis recorded, Stranger In My Own HomeTown is an archetypal Memphis Soul record: rumbling rhythm, parping horn section and strident guitars. The voice apart, it would have been quite at home on any of the real Soul albums that Chips Moman recorded at American, or earlier at Muscle Shoals: anything from Wilson Pickett to Dusty Springfield, from Bobby Womack to Clarence Carter.

It was a minor R&B hit written by Percy Mayfield, a crooner from Houston — a 'Sepia Sinatra', as they were known at the time — whose career flourished lachrymosely at the turn of the 1950s. He sang Cry Baby and Life Is Suicide, but his big hit was 1950's oozing, almost pathetic Please Send Me Someone To Love. When a car crash left him with severe facial injuries, he concentrated on writing, becoming known as 'the poet Laureate of the Blues' and striking up a particularly close relationship with Ray Charles — Hit The Road, Jack and Danger Zone are both his. Stranger In My Own Town was released on Brother Ray's Tangerine label in 1963. 'I'm a poet and my gift is love,' Mayfield once said.

The lyrics to Stranger In My Own Home Town are streaked with self-pity. The singer has been back in town five or six years, he says, but he's still whining about his 'so-called friends' not being 'friendly'. As so often in Elvis' later days — listen to Hurt or Always On My Mind — sloppy childishness brings out the best in him. He never sounds more powerful than he does when wallowing in self-absorption. He has the unmovable grandiosity and solipsism of a real Mama's boy. His deep, bellowing voice really does reshape the universe, putting him at the centre of it — for four and a half minutes, anyway.

A song written by a disfigured black Texan, played by mostly white musicians in a studio that would soon go bankrupt, sung by a dishwater blonde who dyed his hair black and had an alcoholic chimpanzee as a pet — this is the real Memphis Blues.

An American Trilogy

Dixie written by: **Dan Emmett, 1859**
Battle Hymn Of The Republic written by: **Julia Ward Howe, 1861**
All My Trials written by: **unknown**
Arranged: **Mickey Newbury, 1971**
Recorded: **17 February 1972, live concert at Las Vegas Hilton**
First released: **c/w The First Time Ever I Saw Your Face, April 1972**

Hurt is the song which has defined the late Elvis since his death, but An American Trilogy is the one which defined that period during his life. Put together by Country songwriter Mickey Newbury, its arrangement brings together three old tunes in a deliberate, self-conscious conceit. Dixie for the South, Battle Hymn Of The Republic for the North, All My Trials for the Blacks — uniting a country in music at the very time it was falling apart in reality: Vietnam war, ghetto and student riots, Watergate, and the Kennedy and King assassinations.

Beguilingly, the true histories of the individual songs betray even more of the nation's racial, political and sexual complexities.

Dixie, as everyone knows, is a famous old tune written as the anthem of the Confederacy, of white supremacy, of Rhett and Scarlett — and one which long predated the Civil War. Well, no actually. It was a Pop tune, written in New York, on the eve of the Civil War in 1859, by a songwriter and entertainer who was born and died in Ohio, some way north of the Mason-Dixon line. More than that, Dan Emmett was a black-face performer who wrote the tune for his employers, Bryant's Minstrels.

Minstrel shows were enormously popular, with black as well as white Americans, right into the twentieth century. Think of Al Jolson in The Jazz Singer, performing Mammy — I'd walk a million miles for one of your smiles, my mammy. It's the story of a cantor's son exiled from his father pretending to be a black southern son of toil exiled from his homeland, the seemingly disparate personalities united in one body by shared mother love. Truly, as Al Jolson said, you ain't seen nothin' yet.

While hindsight inevitably brands the minstrel show as condescending at best and racist at worst, the briefest consideration prompts harder questions. How could black people have been at all keen on them? One answer, I suppose, is that being born black doesn't mean being born without a sense of self-irony. After all, Jews tell the best Jewish jokes. And if the English can adore a caricatured parody of themselves like Basil Fawlty, it's easy to see how American blacks could relish similar exaggerations of themselves. Also, there is no doubt that a good number of the finest minstrel performers were black — all of whom wore the same, fake black make-up as the white-skinned minstrels.

Another question: if minstrel shows really were so simplistically and blatantly racist in both content and intent, how do you explain their popularity as entertainment? Who'd pay good money for a decent seat in a good Broadway theatre to hear a racist rant? Come to that, if you really hated black people, where's the fun watching someone pretending to be a black person? Particularly if they really are a black person?

Dixie itself points to some of the answers. It's a lament of exile, the song not of a white supremacist who dreams of the delights of old slavery, but of a black who has moved to the North and who dreams of the good life down south. While it almost certainly lied about contemporary blacks' nostalgia for the slave states, its attraction — now as much as then — is the way it taps general human nostalgia, for childhood and simplicity really. (If it had been written by a British composer, it would have been called The Shires, echoing the dreams of

the hordes that flood London's country-bound motorways every Friday evening, and late Sunday night.)

Not that it struck home straight away. In fact, its success began exactly a year later, in April 1860, a year before the start of the Civil War, at the other end of the United States, in New Orleans. Nor did it immediately and permanently become the musical expression of the Confederacy's dreams. That happened only gradually. For some time, it was just a very popular, all-American pop hit. In fact, four days before his assassination, at a White House Party, President Lincoln called for the band to play it. It was only in the post-war period that white supremacists took — with sadly typical ignorance — a slave lament and turned it into a sarabande to their own pernicious history.

The Battle Hymn Of The Republic, by constrast, was deliberately constructed as a patriotic anthem. The tune itself — originally known as Glory Hallelujah — has a surprisingly obscure background.

Although it emerged in the late 1850s — and immediately became very, very popular — no-one has ever been able to prove who wrote it. Every suggestion mooted has later been discredited.

What is known for certain is that within months of the start of the Civil War, it was being sung by northern troops, to words of their own devising. Its first recorded official use was in late 1861, at a flag-raising ceremony for new recruits in Boston. In November of that year, Julia Ward — a pioneer of women's rights — was asked to provide 'a worthier text'. The result was a stirring set of lyrics, not so much warlike as militantly committed to social justice. Hers was not the Civil War of modern history books — a struggle for economic superiority between industrialised capitalist northern states and agrarian, quasi-feudal southern states. Hers was the Civil War of children's history books — a disinterested Northern crusade seeking civil rights for all.

Published as a poem in Atlantic Monthly in February 1862, it quickly became the Unionist anthem of the moment. While Dixie was a kind of Lili Marlene, plangent and obscure enough to work for both sides in the Second World War, The Battle Hymn Of The Republic was unequivocal — a kind of White Cliffs Of Dover of its day. That its attraction persisted after the war would have pleased Julia Ward herself who once commented: 'My poem did some service in the Civil War. I wish very much that it may do good service in the peace.' She would also have been pleased, I imagine, that it provided the title to John Steinbeck's crusading novel The Grapes Of Wrath.

All My Trials, the third part of the Trilogy, which represents Black America, is variously described as a lullaby, a slave song and an old black spiritual. Its lack of accredited authorship certainly indicates that it's probably traditional. Yet its central couplet could as easily be the work of a professional songwriter as an articulate amateur: 'Now, hush, little darlin', don't you cry/You know your daddy's bound to die.' That Elvis started singing it at a time when so many young American men were dying in battle only added to its clear-eyed poignancy.

In his performance of it, the song would end with a reprise of The Battle Hymn Of The

Republic. It's a breathtakingly naive piece of hubris — the notion that he can perform the act of Union with a song in a white, rhinestoned Captain Marvel-like cape, onstage in Las Vegas. 'But it is an illusion,' wrote Greil Marcus in Mystery Train. 'Elvis transcends any real America by evading it. There is no John Brown in his Battle Hymn, no romance in his Dixie, no blood in his slave song. The divisions America shares are simply smoothed away.'

And if Marcus is right, if that's how it felt to an American at the time — how can I ever know for sure? — it would explain something. An American Trilogy was a flop on its first US release. It was on the Billboard Hot 100 just six weeks, never making it higher than number 66, and peaked at 31 on Billboard's easy-listening chart. Even given the generalised slump Elvis was going through, it was a notable failure. Its predecessor, the fairly obscure Until It's Time For You To Go, released in January of the same year, hit number 40 and its immediate successor, August's Burning Love, which hit number two, was his biggest hit between 1969's Suspicious Minds and his death.

But An American Trilogy was a hit in England, reaching number five in June of that year. The easy and probably correct explanation is that the English bought it as a piece of Americana. As Americans come to England and rave about what they imagine is the real England — mostly hokey heritage stuff like red telephone boxes — so the English are suckers for American hokey heritage stuff, notably an Elvis record which seeks to recreate the Civil War and fix the result so everyone wins. The lunatic fringe of English Elvis and Country music fans, a lot of whom live in the badlands of East Anglia — particularly on the Essex/Suffolk border — took An American Trilogy on as their own anthem for Saturday night get-togethers where they'd all dress up as cowboys, firing their toy guns into the air when it was played.

The least charitable, though probably correct, explanation is that these East Anglian cowboys felt the Britain they knew was disappearing and being replaced by a brave new multi-ethnic, multi-cultural world — which they wanted nothing to do with. The supposedly beleaguered Confederacy was a suitably sentimental choice on which to project their emotions. And, to be frank, there weren't that many black people around to tell them not to be so silly and put that Confederate flag away.

Nor, apart from financially, did it make Mickey Newbury a happy man. A Country songwriter from Houston who, a little younger than Elvis, grew up with a similar love of R&B, he wrote the arrangement and recorded it himself first — in a quieter, calmer version than Elvis' deliberately histrionic approach. Best known for straight Country songs — She Even Woke Me Up To Say Goodbye was his biggest hit — Newbury never did anything else remotely like An American Trilogy. And his view of it was remarkably downbeat: 'It was more a detriment than a help because it was not indicative of what I can do.' *ep*

Burning Love

Written by: **Dennis Linde**
Recorded: **28 March 1972, RCA Studio C, Hollywood**
First released: **c/w It's A Matter Of Time, August 1972**

Burning Love was Elvis' only real hit record between 1969's comeback special, Suspicious Minds, and his death. Written and previously recorded by Country guitarist Dennis Linde — who also played on Elvis' version — it sold a million, peaking at number two on the US pop chart. But for some reason, Elvis never really liked it. According to JD Sumner, leader of Elvis' gospelly backing group, the Stamps, 'During the last six years he didn't sing much Rock'n'Roll. He had one song, Burning Love, that he wouldn't sing onstage. Even though the people liked it, he didn't. He preferred to sing songs like My Way or Lord You Gave Me A Mountain.' *ep*

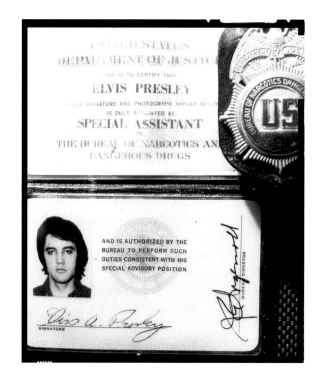

(T is for Trapani in Sicily)

Where I was staying, in a fly-blown hotel, when Elvis died —
and for the Tesco supermarket in Stroud Green Road, London
N4 — which is where I'd do my shopping around the time Elvis
died. Now read this e-mail which I found at
www.elvissightings.com on Thursday, 13 February 1997 at
19:30:58 (EST), posted by Clare Mac mc629@gre.ac.uk:
I saw Elvis this morning at Tesco on Stroud Green Road in
London N4. He was buying some low-fat cottage cheese with
pineapple. He was wearing a shell suit and white socks with red
stripes tucked over the bottom of his trousers!! This proving the
King is alive and well and living near Finsbury Park.
Trapani, Tesco, Thursday — spooky, huh?

Always On My Mind

Written by: **Mark James, Wayne Carson, Johnny Christopher**
Recorded: **27 March 1972, RCA's Studio C, Hollywood**
First released: **c/w Separate Ways, November 1972**

Although it was released as a single in Britain, hitting number nine in December 1972, I can't say I paid this song any attention until the Pet Shop Boys' version of it, which was recorded in 1987 for a US TV show marking the tenth anniversary of Elvis' death. In that version, the emotion was created by the contrast between the open, artless pleading of the lyrics and the blank affectedness of the singing and playing. It was as if deadness had breathed life into it. Somehow, in contrast to most accepted laws of physics, this feeling worked its way back into

the Elvis version. Which is why British Telecom was able to use it for an advert. What was once its vice — lifelessness — has now become its secret source of power. Rather like Elvis himself.

Lyrically, it's a mirrorworld of The Police's Every Breath You Take. Where that song is a serenade of obsessive attention, this is the apologia of someone who is obsessively inattentive — most likely a serial adulterer who can't quite remember how many lovers he's had and which nights he didn't come home. 'I just never took the time,' he sings. 'But you were always on my mind.' Which is just like the Elvis portrayed in Priscilla Presley's memoirs, Elvis And Me. Self-absorbed, he takes her on a small-hours date to the Memphis morgue. Getting religion big time, he starts holding bible readings in their Bel-Air sitting room. 'I sat next to him one evening as he read passages with great force,' she writes. 'Facing us were several of his young female admirers wearing the lowest-cut blouses and the shortest miniskirts ... The sermon stretched to hours, followed by a question-and-answer period during which they vied for his attention.

'Sitting at his feet was an attractive, well-endowed young girl wearing a blouse unbuttoned to her navel. Leaning over seductively, she asked in honeyed tones, "Elvis, do you think the woman at the well was a virgin?" . . . He drew in a deep breath and said, "I like your perfume, honey. What's it called?" "Chanel Number Five," she answered.

'Chanel Number Five? That's what I was wearing! Why didn't he notice it on me?'

With that, she does what any self-respecting woman of her generation would have done: she changes into a new, sexier outfit. When Elvis still doesn't pay attention, she returns to their room and takes an overdose of pills. So hyped up is she, though, that her adrenaline won't even let her get to sleep.

I figure that recording Always On My Mind was Elvis' way of saying: sorry for that evening, honey, but what the hell, I am Elvis, you know.

There is a pleasing symmetry, then, in the knowledge that Elvis and Priscilla — who'd been having an affair with her karate instructor, Mike Stone — had legally separated just a month before it was recorded. Priscilla and Lisa Marie had moved out of the house. Elvis threatened to have Stone killed and became so upset he didn't eat for days.

If that sounds like the story of a Country song, it soon became one. Separate Ways — the a-side of Always On My Mind in the US, the b-side in Britain — really was the inside take on the Presley break-up. One of its two co-writers, Red West, was as inside as you could get. He'd known Elvis since school, been his bodyguard since 1960, married his secretary in 1961 and says he was the one who told Elvis about Priscilla's dalliance with Stone — though Priscilla has also taken credit for that.

Talking about the song, Pet Shop Boy Neil Tennant said, 'It's very much a Country sentiment, that the man should be a bastard.' Unusual though, in ElvisWorld. Given the trumpeted importance of his Country music roots, Elvis recorded surprisingly few Grand Ole Opry style songs — particularly compared with the number of Blues and R&B classics he cut. And those country songs he did record tended to be mawkish standards — For The Good Times, Old Shep — rather than the Drinking & Fucking Someone Else's Wife laments that made Nashville famous. Always On My Mind is the exception. It was cut, in his last but one session at RCA's Hollywood studios, with his usual 1970s back-up band led by James Burton's guitar and coloured by the Gospel voices of JD Sumner and the Stamps. Knowing the state of Elvis' personal life at the time gives the other songs recorded at the three-day session an uncomfortable poignancy. Apart from the big hit, Burning Love, they all told the same story: Separate Ways, For The Good Times (a sad-sack of a Country song about a break-up written by Kris Kristofferson: 'make believe you love me one more time') Where Do I Go From Here, Fool (written by, of all people, James Last), Always On My Mind and It's A Matter Of Time.

It wasn't, of course. The Virgin Bride had left the Sun King's palace, never to return. *ep*

(U is for Uncle Silas Payne)

An old, blind, black man who worked on Sam Phillips' father's farm outside Florence, Alabama. He taught young Sam about music, about the power of what Sam later called 'genuine, untutored Negro' music. When Sam started his own record company he remembered what Uncle Silas had taught him and went looking for 'Negroes with mud on their boots and patches in their overalls, battered instruments and unfettered techniques'. He found them and recorded them. Then he found Elvis and taught him what Uncle Silas had taught him. As has often been said, Uncle Silas is the secret hero of the whole story.

Promised Land
Written by: **Chuck Berry**
Recorded: **15 December 1973, Stax Studios, Memphis**
First released: **c/w It's Midnight, October 1974**

The jailhouse song of all jailhouse songs, Promised Land was written by Chuck Berry while he was locked up for transporting an under-age female across a state border. While the trial was undoubtedly a racist set-up, his claims of innocence were somewhat undermined by a later conviction for installing spy cameras in the women's toilets of his amusement park — at the bottom of the bowls, with the lenses pointing upwards. Its title is an immediately obvious mix of jail-cell wishes and Gospel-song memories. Promised Land, written in 1963, was Chuck Berry's last great composition, and became one of the last real hits of his career. Soon after, he retreated into self-revivalism, drowning his talent in cynicism and bitterness. It tells the story of a young man's cross-country trip from Norfolk, Virginia to Los Angeles. Allegedly, although Chuck had spent many years on the road, he'd never done this particular journey and had to ask a prison warder for a map to check it on. Of course — or so the story goes — the warder suspected a jailbreak and took some convincing. Starting point apart, it's the story of Elvis' life — something acknowledged by Merle Haggard in From Graceland To The Promised Land, which English professor Linda Ray Pratt described as 'the perfect Southern folk song about Elvis'. It was recorded a couple of months after his divorce — which came through on 10 October 10, 1973 — and was one of the last songs cut at his final studio session in Memphis — after this he used Graceland. It was at the Stax studios, the converted cinema in the black part of town where so many great black soul stars had recorded. Two sets of exceptional studio musicians were on hand — both the original Stax rhythm section of drummer Al Jackson, bassist Duck Dunn, and a pair of the Muscle Shoals regulars he'd worked with at American Studios back in 1959, guitarist Reggie Young and bassist Tommy Cogbill. It should have produced something special. But it didn't. Even when Elvis' regular band, led by James Burton, was brought in. One big hit, My Boy, came out of the eight-day session but really the only track that counts is Promised Land. It was apparently cut at the end of the same kind of loose practice session which had produced so many other hits for him over the years. He'd been singing Chuck Berry since 1955, when he performed Maybellene on the Louisiana Hayride radio show, but his versions of Memphis, Tennessee and Too Much Monkey Business had both been oddly unhappy — the latter makes an uncomfortable-sounding contemporary reference to the Vietnam War.

On Promised Land, though, he roars right into the song and straight through it, holding on for dear life. He never again sounded like he had a future.

(V is for Voodoo)

In 1956, The Catholic Sun described Elvis' music as a 'voodoo of frustration and defiance'.

Hurt

Written by: **Jimmie Craine, Al Jacobs**
Recorded: **5–6 February 1976, Graceland**
First released: **c/w For The Heart, March 1976**

Little noticed in Elvis' lifetime, or for some time after, Hurt has become the touchstone song for the obsessive wing of Elvis fandom, a favourite of Elvis impersonators everywhere and the theme tune of Death Week, the annual ritual venerations of Elvis which have developed around the candlelight ceremony marking his death on 16 August.

There are cod-religious Elvis movements: the Church of Elvis; the Eighth Day Transfiguration Cult; the First Church of Jesus Christ; the First Presleyterian Church of Elvis The Divine, 'the only religion that will matter in the next millennium'. But to Death Week celebrants, such irony is blasphemy. The Elvis worshipped by these 'true' fans is not the young Memphis Flash or the smooth, polished screen idol but the fat drug addict halfway to hamburger heaven who staggered around the stage, giggling through his own hits, mutilating the glories of his own history. Self-absorbed as ever, Fat Elvis didn't so much turn his pain into performance as make the pain the performance. The immediacy and visibility of his downward spiral turned his concerts into a kind of Oprah Winfrey show as directed by Vincente Minelli — with the real Elvisiana mystery revealing itself in Hurt.

It would be very easy to suggest that the 'true' fans see in the late Fat Elvis a reflection of their own lives, their own pain. But it would probably be right. This is Elvis as patron saint of trailer-park misery — and incomprehension.

Previously a 1945 hit for (black) Roy Hamilton and a 1961 hit for (white) Timi Yuro, Hurt was recorded in Graceland's Jungle Room, with its green carpeted floor and its matching green carpeted ceiling. (The guide tells you that ceiling carpets were a popular interior decor choice of the 1970s and you perhaps believe him.) Elvis' mood at the all-night session is easily judged by the choice of songs. It's a checklist of sorrow and humiliation: She Thinks I Still Care, The Last Farewell, Danny Boy, Solitaire, Moody Blue. Throughout his career, Elvis was obsessed with one question: why me? But the meaning of the question changed over the years, from what did I do to deserve all this fame, wealth and glory, to what did I do to deserve all this unhappiness? The solipsism of the second question is both its tragedy and its power — it's how Elvis saw it, and how the 'true' fans feel it.

Hurt — which Elvis also sang at his last recorded show, in Rapid City, on 21 June 1977 — is not much of a song, to be honest. The cry of a cuckold, its only draw is the directness with which it expresses pain — mostly by repeating the word 'hurt' over and over again. *ep*

(W is for Red West)

Was he the most important man in Elvis' life? Red West says they were best friends at Humes High and that he saved Elvis from getting beaten up by football players angered by his haircut. 'I really felt sorry for him,' said Red. 'He seemed very lonely and had no real friends.' He worked as Elvis' bodyguard in the early Sun days. When Elvis joined the army, Red went with him to Germany. When he left, Red and his cousin Sonny were taken on as bodyguards and full-time founder members of the Memphis Mafia.

According to some sources, in 1961 Elvis commissioned Red to write his first professional composition, That's Someone You Never Forget, a song about the most important woman in his life — his mother. (In all, Elvis recorded eight of his songs.) West says he was the one who told Elvis that Priscilla was having an affair with her karate teacher, Mike Stone. At which point, Elvis asked Red to hire a hit man to kill her. He hired one for $10,000 — he says — but Elvis changed his mind, and decided not to have his wife murdered. Next, Red wrote a song about the break-up, Separate Ways, and gave it to Elvis who made it the title track of his next album.

Either because he'd been beating up Elvis fans or because he was helping service Elvis with drugs, he was fired by Vernon Presley on 13 July 1976 — along with Sonny and another bodyguard member of the Memphis Mafia, Dave Hebler. Their revenge was to write the first exposé of their former boss's junkiedom, Elvis — What Happened?. Elvis heard about the book and tried to buy them off. When that failed he addressed the problem at his very last Las Vegas show, on 2 December 1976, in a monologue to the audience — who, as the revelations were not yet public, can have had little idea what he was on about. It was Elvis at his most fork- tongued. 'I've just returned from New York where I attended a meeting of the International Federation Of Narcotics Agents and I've been awarded honorary membership, ladies and gentlemen. I don't pay any attention to movie magazines or newspapers because in my case they make the stories up. When I hear the rumours flying around, I get sick. In this day and age, you can't even get sick. They said I was strung out on heroin and I've never been strung out on anything but music. If I ever find out who started that I'll knock their goddam head off, the son of a bitch. That is dangerous to me, my family, my friends and my little girl. If I find out who started this, maids or room clerks or freaks that carry your luggage up, I'll rip their tongues out by the roots! Now I'll sing Blue Hawaii from the movie.'

When it came time to promote the book, Red was forthright. Elvis, he said, 'takes pills to go to sleep. He takes pills to get up. He takes pills to go to the john.' In another, Hebler said of Elvis: 'It seems he is bent on death.' The book was published on 1 August 1977. Fifteen days later, Elvis was dead.

Way Down
Written by: **Layng Martine Jr**
Recorded: **30 October 1976, Graceland**
First released: **c/w Pledging My Love, June 1977**

Way Down was climbing the charts as Elvis died, one of four songs he cut in his last studio recording session, in Graceland's Jungle Room, with its acoustically helpful carpeted ceiling. As Elvis turned in on himself towards death, so he took his music with him. In 1973 he took to recording at Stax on McLemore Avenue, in the heart of Memphis' central black ghetto — soon after which Stax went bankrupt. From then on, when it came time to record, he only left the city one more time — RCA Hollywood, March 1975.

He cut four songs at this session. Their titles have an undeniable poignancy. The first, It's Easy For You, was, believe it or not, an Andrew Lloyd-Webber/Tim Rice song. Next came Way Down itself. Driven by James Burton's scampering guitar, it's almost a duet with the bass voice of JD Sumner, leader of Elvis' backing group —

to whom Elvis had recently given a brand-new white Lincoln Continental, a $40,000 diamond ring and a $4,000 watch. More than that, Elvis was such a fan of Sumner's that he gave him and his group label credit on Way Down. It reads: Vocal Acc by JD Sumner & The Stamps QT, K Westmoreland, S Nielsen and M. Smith.

Then came Way Down's flip side, Pledging My Love, a big hit for the R&B star hymned by Paul Simon as 'the late, great Johnny Ace' who died backstage in Houston, playing Russian roulette, on 25 December 1955. Elvis spent that Christmas quietly at home with his parents, five days after recording his third single — it was the last regular Christmas he'd ever know, of course.

The very last studio song Elvis recorded was an old country number, a hit for Jim Reeves: He'll Have To Go.

PS. Five weeks later, alone in a Las Vegas penthouse, Elvis wrote a note to himself, which was found by a cleaner and auctioned at Sotheby's in June 1991. It read: 'I feel so alone sometimes. The night is quiet for me. I would love to be able to sleep. I am glad everyone is gone now. I will probably not rest tonight. I have no need for all of this. Help me, Lord.' *ep*

ELVIS MUG Fine bone china, made in England, 'hand-painted' splashy blue and orange image of the King and his castle (Graceland, that is). Produced in 1991, by Mac Products.

ELVIS STAMP Just 29 cents worth of it, issued on 5 January 1993 by the US Postal Service and dreamed up by then Postmaster General Anthony Frank. A lurid painting by Mark Stutzman, the design finally chosen — by the American public, in a ballot — featured the young Memphis Flash Elvis. The old Fat Elvis version was rejected out of hand. Even Bill Clinton voted for the young Elvis.

ELVIS CLOCK A foot-high Elvis in high 1950s pomp, with the legs acting as a swinging pendulum for the clock. Came out in 1992 and has since been bootlegged right across the world.

ELVIS WATCH with a black leather strap and a face which has the King at the mic in pink jacket, black pegs and white socks. Manufactured by Fossil, it comes with a one-year warranty and in a neat metal box — a pink saloon with Elvis at the wheel and a Graceland Or Bust! sign on the back window. Like a lot of Elvis memorabilia, it also features the King's 1970s logo, the letters TCB, with a zig-zag line going through them. This is meant to stand for Taking Care Of Business . . . In A Flash. June Juanico (see J is for June Juanico, in the Elvis Alphabet), has a different view. In her book she describes how when she was dating Elvis, he took to using acronyms for swear words or risque thoughts. He referred to the Memphis Mafia as CBs — ie 'cherry busters' or deflowerers of virgins. She then writes: 'When Elvis adopted the TCB logo in later years, I had to laugh. Knowing how he loved an inside joke, I knew it couldn't stand for Taking Care Of Business; if so, he would have included the O.'

ELVIS GREETING CARD A 'recycled paper' cut-out of the late Elvis, produced by Paper House Productions in Woodstock of all places. A small note on Elvis' back informs us that Elvis' 'unique costumes became classics of the 1970s style, copied by many entertainers of that era'. But these royal raiments were fit really for only one person — The King.

ELVIS SHIRT High quality, second-hand short-sleeve shirts with an Elvis Presley flash on one breast pocket and on the other, one for Crown Electric, where Elvis worked as a truck driver. Available at Graceland.

ELVIS PLATE Elvis' Birthplace: Tupelo Mississippi by Diane Sivavec, plate 2 in the limited edition of In The Footsteps Of The King. Issued in 1993, it carries the announcement: 'Pigments required may poison food'. So, no two pounds of burnt bacon and a couple of fried peanut butter and banana sandwiches tonight, then.

ELVIS CALENDAR Elvis: The Wertheimer Collection. Twelve months of beautifully printed reproductions of pictures from Wertheimer's book, Elvis '56. August shows Elvis at the moment of his triumphant return to Memphis, performing live on Independence Day 1956.

(X is for X-ray)

In 1957, the American magazine Harper's reported that in Russia, bootleg Elvis records, cut on hospital X-ray plates were selling for $12.50 each. This story has been repeated verbatim ever since. Wondering how you cut recorded music into something as hard as a glass X-ray plate, I called a leading expert in record cutting at his London studio. He confirmed my doubts in two words from the start of the alphabet. A was for 'absolute' and B was for 'bollocks'.

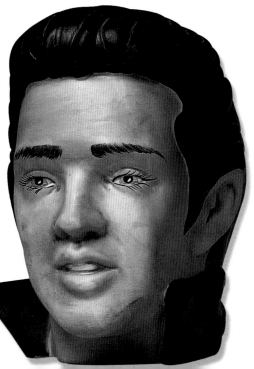

ELVIS BUST Definitely a bootleg, found in a shop in north London. Spookily, it was not far from the Tesco supermarket where Elvis was spotted in early 1997 (see Elvis Alphabet).

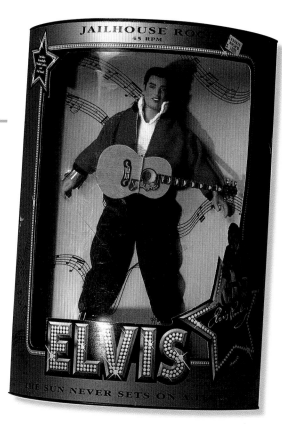

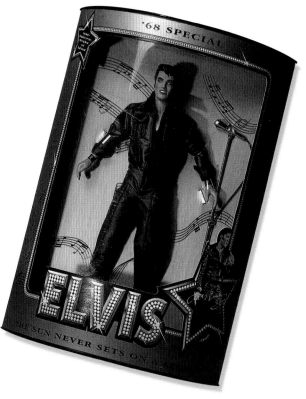

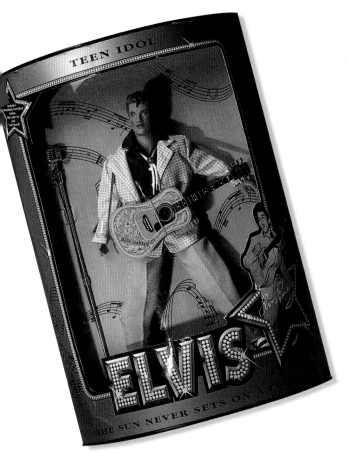

ELVIS DOLLS The early ones, with blue suede shoes and a checked shirt, are rare and valuable. But the 1994 ones are suitably shlocky. There is a choice of three Elvises. Jailhouse Rock has him in red windbreaker and white shirt. For Teen Idol he is in pink jacket and grey pegs. And the '68 Special is Elvis in black leather. All three boxes feature the same line: 'The sun never sets on a legend.'

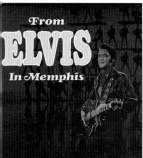

The ten essential currently available Elvis CDs (in as close to chronological order as you can get):

The Sun Sessions CD
Elvis '56
Complete 50s Masters The King Of Rock'n'Roll (five CD set)
Elvis' Christmas album
Elvis Is Back
Essential 60s Masters: From Nashville To Memphis (five CD set)
NBC–TV Special (The 1968 Comeback album)
From Elvis In Memphis
Essential 70s Masters: Walk A Mile In My Shoes (five CD set)
Amazing Grace: His Greatest Sacred Performances (two CD set)

That there is no greatest hits package in that list is not snobbery but recognition that the currently available ones just aren't up to scratch. The best I've seen is the 1978 double album Elvis' 40 Greatest, in a 'special pink pressing' — despite the fact that it doesn't include a single Sun track (or Little Sister) and that, because it's simply a reissue of a 1974 collection, stops short of Elvis' last few hits.

There are also three other excellent discontinued Elvis collections:

Elvis Presley Sings Leiber & Stoller does just what it says on the labels: collects together every Jerry Leiber and Mike Stoller song that Elvis every recorded.

Reconsider Baby should have been called Elvis Sings The Blues. Released in 1985, on blue vinyl, it brings together twelve of Elvis' best R&B covers. Among them are the first issue of the string-free Tomorrow Night, the original, uncensored version of One Night and a completely different mix of Stranger In My Own Home Town, incomparably superior to the only version now available — which has been so badly mastered that the drums are heavily distorted.

The Complete Sun Sessions is the vinyl version of The Sun Sessions CD and has six more tracks, though admittedly, they are nothing more significant than extra out-takes of I Love You Because and I'm Left, You're Right, She's Gone. At the time of its issue, 1987, this really did seem like it collected all of Elvis' professional recordings for Sun. Then 1992's Complete Fifties Masters turned up three more tracks — the Clovers' Fool, Fool, Fool and Joe Turner's Shake, Rattle And Roll, both recorded as demos in a Lubbock, Texas studio, and the first, country-style take of Blue Moon. Cynics expect further tracks to surface. *ep*

The ten best Elvis cover versions:

1. Always On My Mind/Pet Shop Boys
2. Viva Las Vegas/ZZ Top
3. Can't Help Falling In Love/Bono
4. Suspicious Minds/Candi Staton
5. That's All Right (Mama)/Marty Robbins
6. Little Sister/Ry Cooder
7. Blue Hawaii/Willie Nelson
8. Only The Strong Survive/Frankie Knuckles
9. Mystery Train/The Band
10. True Love Travels On A Gravel Road/Nick Lowe *ep*

(Y is for Yoga)

Is As Yoga Does, a song featured in Easy Come, Easy Go, the first of the three 1967 Elvis films — it features an encounter with some hippies, which explains the modish subject matter. He played a frogman and sang it as a duet with Elsa Lanchester, an actress previously linked with Frankenstein (she played the monster's bride in The Bride Of Frankenstein) and Charles Laughton (she was both his fictional wife, Anne of Cleves in his Private Life Of Henry VIII and his real wife). Laughton was also linked with Elvis. He was the substitute host on Elvis' first appearance on The Ed Sullivan Show — Sullivan was recovering from a car accident — on 9 September 1956. Elvis sang Don't Be Cruel and after he'd finished Laughton commented, laughingly: 'Well, what did someone say? Music hath charms to soothe the savage breast?' Laughton died in 1962. In 1964 Elsa Lanchester acted in Mary Poppins. In 1986, she was in Die Laughing — and then died. Elvis recorded many other strikingly titled songs, most of them for his movies and many of them collected on the bootleg album Elvis' Greatest Shit! (Dog Vomit, Sux 005, 1984): Dominic The Impotent Bull, Smorgasbord, Queenie Wahini's Papaya, Petunia The Gardener's Daughter, Fort Lauderdale Chamber Of Commerce, There's No Room To Rhumba In A Sports Car and You Can't Say No In Acapulco — the last pair both being cut on the same memorable January day in 1963.

Elvis by Albert Goldman, McGraw-Hill, 1981
Elvis: The Last 24 Hours by Albert Goldman, St Martin's Press, 1991
Portrait of the artist as ageing, racist voyeur, addicted to pharmaceutical morphine and peanut butter. To the true believer, Goldman is the anti-Christ, purveyor of filth and lies. To the sceptical fan, he's got all the details right while completely missing the overall picture. There has never been a serious challenge to his research but the book never gets to grips with the most obvious of its own rationales: if Elvis was so stupidly unimportant, why did the publishers think it worth paying such a vast advance? But the book's unrelenting dyspepsia does have its own artistic integrity. There's a kind of fascination to reading Goldman's obsessive rantings and a perverse syllogistic logic to his central aesthetic judgment: that Elvis was a non-talent because he wasn't black. Goldman's emotional extension of this is: and that was Elvis' own fault!
That Goldman himself choked to death on the free food of a first-class airline flight is one of fate's more vulgar jokes.

Mystery Train by Greil Marcus, Omnibus, 1977
It's old — written while Elvis was alive. It's not just about Elvis — there are three other major essays in it, on The Band, Sly Stone and Randy Newman (well before his Toy Story days, naturally). It's too often pretentious — even such an original brain and fine write as Greil Marcus should forebear sharing his dreams and daydreams with the reader. And yet it's still one of the best things ever published about Elvis. The selective discography was ground-breakingly intelligent and informative when it was first published and it's still the best beginner's guide both to the highlights of Elvis' own career and to the Blues and Country music that stood behind his innovations.
The long essay on Elvis — which came out at a time when his career was at an all-time nadir — offered the first detailed chronicle of the Sun recordings, the first reconsideration of his later work and a string of bright, sharp comments. A single example: 'To Elvis, Watergate would have been something like a cosmic paternity suit.' As with a lot of Marcus' stuff, it's not even a case of not being sure if I agree with it so much as not even having a clue what he's on about. But it sounds like it means something. And it made me laugh.

Graceland: The Living Legacy Of Elvis Presley, by Chet Flippo, Hamlyn, 1994
The Homes & Gardens version of the King's life. Lavishly lifeless photographs of Graceland's decor and the contents of the Elvis collections on the other side of Elvis Presley Boulevard. An excellent reminder of the truly fabulous vulgarity of Graceland, with scalpel-sharp text by Flippo. Just one thing is missing, of course. A picture of the toilet where he died.

Elvis In His Own Words by Mick Farren and Pearce Marchbank, Omnibus, 1977
A quickie post-death book of real quality. Lots and lots of black and white photographs arranged and displayed by one of Britain's best graphic designers and annotated by one of Britain's best music journalists. The rest is just what it says in the title — Elvis' very few interviews arranged in chronological order to produce something like a mini-autobiography.

Last Train To Memphis by Peter Guralnick, Little, Brown, 1994

As warm and loving as Goldman is bitter and twisted. Where Goldman's Elvis is a half-wit who lucked out, Guralnick's is a singer who knew what he was trying to do and worked hard at it, in the studio at least, effectively becoming the first self-produced pop performer.

So much serious (and ironic) Elvis commentary is based on duality. On one hand, the drug addict, on the other, the honorary narcotics agent. Lover of heavy-bodied Mama Gladys — and of porno vids featuring heavy-bodied Gladys-like Mama figures fighting like hell-cats. The vibrant young iconoclast versus the ageing, bloated everyman. And, above all, the original duality, Elvis and his stillborn twin, Jesse. Whatever the merits of Guralnick's book — and they are overwhelming — it can also be read as the good twin to the bad twin of Goldman's Elvis. The two portraits of the subject are Manicheistically different enough to make hardened doubters believe in parallel universes — the Sun King versus the Scum King.

Erudite, sweet-hearted and exhaustive — not to say occasionally exhausting — Guralnick's book takes the story up to Elvis' departure for Germany in September 1958. The second volume will finish the story. Which is a telling fact — four years of Elvis' artistic career in the first book, the remaining nineteen squashed into the other. Aesthetically justified or not, it highlights Guralnick's uneasiness at dealing with Pop. Sometimes you can't help but feel he overvalues sincerity, honesty and authenticity at the expense of Pop's other life-affirming demons, lust, avarice, exhibitionism. To put it another way, he wouldn't know a great jacket if you bought it for him. The evil twin doesn't get a look-in.

The Two Kings by AJ Jacobs, Pavilion, 1994

In 1974, according to his haidresser, Elvis said he believed he was Jesus Christ. This beauteous blasphemy highlights the 'uncanny' similarities between Elvis and Jesus. 'Jesus was a carpenter' it states. Then: 'Elvis majored in woodwork.' And both, of course, made famous, unexpected comebacks. Jesus, in Jerusalem to Mary Magdalene, three days after his apparent death on Calvary; Elvis, in Burbank, to millions of TV viewers five years after his apparent artistic death in Hollywood. A better worked and more plausible conceit than Don DeLillo's in White Noise — Elvis and Hitler, they were both Mama's boys.

The Elvis Reader: Texts And Sources On The King Of Rock'n'Roll, ed. Kevin Quain, St Martin's Press, 1992

A collection which successfully straddles an uncomfortable divide — academia and journalism. It includes both some of the best well-known writing on Elvis — extracts from the Goldman book, Lester Bangs' Where Were You When Elvis Died?, Stanley Booth's A Hound Dog, To The Manor Born — and some of the undeservedly obscure — notably a couple of very early pieces from Harper's magazine. Its taste is fine, though perhaps a little predictable, and its sweep wide, though perhaps a little heavy on Elvis' death.

❰ Z is for Also Sprach Zarathustra ❱

The music to which Elvis arrived onstage in his 1970s concerts — its first appearance seems to have been his New York live debut, at Madison Square Garden, on 10 June, 1972. The first song he played that night was his first single, That's All Right.

Given modern fame by its use in the film 2001: A Space Odyssey, Also Sprach Zarathustra is a tone poem by German composer Richard Strauss (1864-1949). He wrote it in 1896, using twelve-note material twelve years before Schoenberg. Originally subtitled 'Symphonic optimism in fin-de-siécle form dedicated to the 20th Century', it depicts the 'division between nature and men and the attempt to liberate the individual through laughter'. This portrait is elaborated, in the composer's words, by alternating the two remotest keys, C Major , which represents nature, and B Major, which stands for humanity, then bringing them together at the end of the piece. The opening theme (which is all you got to hear at an Elvis concert) was described by Strauss thus: 'The sun rises. The individual enters the world or the world enters the individual.' (Sun? Individual entering the world? On your marks, Elvis academics and conspiracy theorists.)

Strauss was paid 3,200 marks for writing it. It was 'freely based' on the epic prose poem of the same name by German philosopher Friedrich Nietzsche (1844-1900), one of whose tenets was Only The Strong Survive — a thesis elaborated by Elvis on his 1969 version of the Jerry Butler song. He also wrote about the importance of the 'Dionysian value-standard'. Many commentators have pointed to the similarity between the atmosphere of early Elvis shows and Dionysian ritual celebrations in ancient Greece. Van K Brock, for example, in Images Of Elvis, The South And America, wrote that 'Pentecostalism, like Rock, is a Dionysian cult; offering similar ecstatic release in response to frenzied stimuli'. But the core of Nietzsche's thought, and the one that earned him the blame for providing philosophical and moral underpinning for Nazism, was the concept of the Ubermensch. There is no evidence that Elvis ever studied Nietzsche — which is perhaps surprising given his interest in books of metaphysical pensees such as, according to hairdresser and 'intimate spiritual adviser' Larry Geller, The Impersonal Life by Joseph Benner. But it is easy to imagine him sitting on the toilet in Graceland pondering Nietzsche's dream of 'the possibility of the emergence of exceptional human beings capable of an independence and creativity elevating them beyond the level of the general human rule'. Like Elvis, Nietzsche died young (fifty six) and spent the last part of his life in seclusion — though in his case it was twelve years in a mental hospital, his brain destroyed by the syphilis which would kill him four years after Strauss's work appeared:

So what was so significant to Elvis about this piece of music that he chose it as his theme tune? Ed Parker, one of Elvis' spiritual 'mentors' and karate instructors. told Brock, 'that as far as he knew Elvis simply liked the movements and rhythm of the music.'

Private Elvis by Diego Cortez, FEY, 1978

The first arty wacko Elvis book, it came out soon enough after his death to retain a breath of originality. It was launched, in New York, with a real downtown art show — everyone dressed in black, a high ratio of junkies and friends of Brian Eno's, maps on the wall seeking to 'demonstrate' the weird topological similarity between Memphis and Stuttgart. Even without the surrounding arty hoopla, the pictures themselves are striking enough — b/ws of Elvis in the army. Girls hang on his arm expectantly, mouths open with sexual possibilities. These candid, revelatory narratives are given added depth by the knowledge that, at the same time, Elvis had yet another, even more private life. He was courting the 14-year-old daughter of one of his senior officers, the future virgin(ish) bride, Priscilla. By contrast, these greasy snapshots with semi-professional German girls make him seem an almost-normal young man on the prowl.

Elvis '56: In The Beginning by Alfred Wertheimer, Collier, 1979

A photo-realist employed by RCA to take candid promo shots of their new star, Wertheimer took 3,800 photographs of Elvis over a period of two years. The best of them, collected in this book, comprise an astounding portrait of the artist as young sex star, full of distractingly rich detail. For example, there's one of Elvis on the Chattanooga choo-choo to Memphis on Independence Day, 1956 in which you find yourself drawn as much by Elvis' matching ring and watch band as by his intense stare. Another, more obvious example, perhaps the best-known of all the photographs has Elvis backstage with a gorgeous young girl, their tongues touching, half in play, half in lust. You can't help but find yourself wondering: what happened next? And what did she do with the rest of her life?

The Hitchhiker's Guide To Elvis by Mick Farren, The Book Press, 1994

As Farren points out in his introduction, he first heard Elvis in 1956 and has never been the same since. It's an alphabetical catalogue of Elvisiana. Where else would you see — recorded with equal parts reverence and irreverence — the fact that Elvis hated fish so much he wouldn't let his wife eat it while he was around? Or find the code words Elvis gave women to use so they were put straight through to him when they called Graceland. Ann-Margaret was Thumper and Ursula Andress was Alan. Fish phobia? Naming one of the world's sexiest women after a Disney rabbit? Let us be honest, a French psychoanalyst could base an entire career on exploring such strangeness.

The Truth About Elvis by Jess Stearn with Larry Geller, Jove paperback, 1980

I put this in because a) a book written by a hairdresser-cum-spiritual-adviser is simply irresistible — its vulgarity is its grace b) it has a fabulously stupid painting of Elvis on the cover. Double-breasted, four-button-show white suit with lapels the size of albatross wings and flares as wide as the Pacific. With the sun pretending to be a halo behind his head, Elvis looks down, humbly, and stretches out his hands like Jesus gathering up his flock. The final touch is the flash of lightning running from his right hand down into the clouds. Part echo of the 1970s Elvis logo, Taking Care of Business — In A Flash. And part reference to the famous Michelangelo painting. *ep*

credits

Bibliography

Aspects of Elvis: Tryin' To Get To You
eds Alan Clayson and Spencer Leigh, Sidgwick & Jackson, 1994

Dead Elvis: A Chronicle Of A Cultural Obsession
Greil Marcus, Anchor, 1992

The Complete Guide To The Music Of Elvis Presley
John Robertson, Omnibus Press, 1994

Elvis: A Biography
Jerry Hopkins, Simon & Schuster, 1972

Elvis And Me
Priscilla Beaulieu Presley with Sandra Harmon, Putnam, 1985

Elvis: The Complete Illustrated Record
Roy Carr and Mick Farren, Eel Pie, 1982

Elvis In The Twilight of Memory
June Juanico, Little, Brown, 1997

The Elvis Encyclopedia
David E Stanley with Frank Coffey, Virgin, 1994

Elvis: The Final Years
Jerry Hopkins, St Martin's Press, 1981

Mondo Elvis: A Collection of Stories and Poems
eds Richard Peabody and Lucinda Ebersole, St Martin's Press, 1994

The Ultimate Elvis
Patricia Jobe Pierce, Simon & Schuster, 1994

Sources

Various newspapers and magazines, notably: **The New York Sunday Times Magazine, the Mail On Sunday, the Guardian, the Observer, the New Yorker, Mojo, 78 Quarterly, Rolling Stone**

Sleevenotes

The Complete 50s Masters: The King Of Rock'n'Roll
Peter Guralnick

The Essential 60s Masters: From Nashville To Memphis Peter Guralnick

The Essential 70s Masters: Walk A Mile In My Shoes
Dave Marsh

Elvis Presley Sings Leiber & Stoller
Jerry Leiber and Mike Stoller

The Memphis Record Peter Guralnick

The Sun Sessions Roy Carr

The Complete Sun Sessions Peter Guralnick

Leiber & Stoller: Only In America Atlantic, Robert Palmer

Mean Old World: The Blues From 1940 To 1994
Four CD set, The Smithsonian Collection by Lawrence Hoffman

Sun Records: The Blues Years 1950–1956
Nine CD set, Charly, ed Martin Hawkins

The Sun Box Charly, Colin Escott and Martin Hawkins

Further reading

Lost Highways: Journeys & Arrivals Of American Musicians Peter Guralnick, Godine, 1979

The Faber Companion To 20th Century Popular Music Phil Hardy and Dave Laing, Faber, 1995

I Am The Blues Willie Dixon with Don Snowden, Quartet, 1989

The Heart Of Rock And Soul Dave Marsh, Plume, 1989

Encyclopedia of Pop, Rock and Soul Irwin Stambler, St Martin's Press, 1974

Guinness Book Of British Hit Singles Paul Gambaccini, Tim Rice, Jo Rice, Guinness

What Was The First Rock'n'Roll Record? Jim Dawson and Steve Propes, Faber and Faber, 1992

Country Nick Tosches, Scribners, 1985

Unsung Heroes of Rock'n'Roll Nick Tosches, Scribners, 1984

Sweet Soul Music Peter Guralnick, Virgin, 1986

You Send Me: The Life And Times Of Sam Cooke Daniel Wolff, Morrow, 1995

Hit Men Fredric Dannen, Vintage, 1991

Lives Of The Great Songs ed Tim De Lisle, Pavilion, 1994

Dancing In The Street Robert Palmer, BBC, 1996

Feel Like Going Home: Portraits in Blues and Rock'n'Roll Peter Guralnick, Omnibus, 1978

The Most Southern Place On Earth James C Cobb, Oxford, 1992

Honkers And Shouters Arnold Shaw, Collier, 1978

Walking To New Orleans John Broven, Blues Unlimited, 1974

Ghosts Of Mississippi Maryanne Vollers, Bay Back, 1995

Making Tracks Charlie Gillett, WH Allen, 1975

The Sound Of The City Charlie Gillett, Sphere, 1971

Showtime At The Apollo Ted Fox, Quartet, 1985

Baby That Was Rock & Roll Robert Palmer and John Lahr, Harvest, 1978

The History Of The Blues Francis Davis, Hyperion, 1995

Jane and Michael Stern's Encyclopedia Of Pop Culture HarperPerennial, 1992

The Guinness Encyclopedia Of Popular Music ed Colin Larkin Guinness, 1992

The New Grove Dictionary of American Music ed H Wiley Hitchcock and Stanley Sadie, MacMillan, 1986

Deep Blues Robert Palmer, Penguin, 1982

Black Sea: The Birthplace Of Civilisation And Barbarism Neal Ascherson, Vintage, 1996

Land Where The Blues Began Alan Lomax, Delta, 1993

Juke Joint Birney Imes, University Of Mississippi Press, 1990

Ancient And Modern William Eggleston, Jonathan Cape, 1992

ep